Racism

Other titles in the Hot Topics series include:

Racism

by David Robson

LUCENT BOOKS
A part of Gale, Cengage Learning

Detroit • New York • San Francisco • New Haven, Conn • Waterville, Maine • London

GALE
CENGAGE Learning™

LIBRARY OF CONGRESS CATALOGING-IN-PUBLICATION DATA

Robson, David, 1966–
  Racism / by David Robson.
    p. cm. -- (Hot topics)
  Includes bibliographical references and index.
  ISBN 978-1-4205-0228-2 (hardcover)
  1. United States--Race relations. 2. Racism--United States--History.
I. Title.
  E185.61.R688 2010
  305.800973--dc22

                                                                2010016846

Lucent Books
27500 Drake Rd.
Farmington Hills, MI 48331

ISBN-13: 978-1-4205-0228-2
ISBN-10: 1-4205-0228-X

Printed in the United States of America
1 2 3 4 5 6 7 14 13 12 11 10

Printed by Bang Printing, Brainerd, MN, 1ˢᵗ Ptg., 10/2010

CONTENTS

FOREWORD

Young people today are bombarded with information. Aside from traditional sources such as newspapers, television, and the radio, they are inundated with a nearly continuous stream of data from electronic media. They send and receive e-mails and instant messages, read and write online "blogs," participate in chat rooms and forums, and surf the Web for hours. This trend is likely to continue. As Patricia Senn Breivik, the former dean of university libraries at Wayne State University in Detroit, has stated, "Information overload will only increase in the future. By 2020, for example, the available body of information is expected to double every 73 days! How will these students find the information they need in this coming tidal wave of information?"

Ironically, this overabundance of information can actually impede efforts to understand complex issues. Whether the topic is abortion, the death penalty, gay rights, or obesity, the deluge of fact and opinion that floods the print and electronic media is overwhelming. The news media report the results of polls and studies that contradict one another. Cable news shows, talk radio programs, and newspaper editorials promote narrow viewpoints and omit facts that challenge their own political biases. The World Wide Web is an electronic minefield where legitimate scholars compete with the postings of ordinary citizens who may or may not be well-informed or capable of reasoned argument. At times, strongly worded testimonials and opinion pieces both in print and electronic media are presented as factual accounts.

Conflicting quotes and statistics can confuse even the most diligent researchers. A good example of this is the question of whether or not the death penalty deters crime. For instance, one study found that murders decreased by nearly one-third when the death penalty was reinstated in New York in 1995. Death penalty supporters cite this finding to support their argument that the existence of the death penalty deters criminals from committing murder. However, another study found that states without the death penalty have murder rates below the national average. This study is cited by opponents of capital punishment, who reject the claim that the death penalty deters murder. Students need context and clear, informed discussion if they are to think critically and make informed decisions.

The Hot Topics series is designed to help young people wade through the glut of fact, opinion, and rhetoric so that they can think critically about controversial issues. Only by reading and thinking critically will they be able to formulate a viewpoint that is not simply the parroted views of others. Each volume of the series focuses on one of today's most pressing social issues and provides a balanced overview of the topic. Carefully crafted narrative, fully documented primary and secondary source quotes, informative sidebars, and study questions all provide excellent starting points for research and discussion. Full-color photographs and charts enhance all volumes in the series. With its many useful features, the Hot Topics series is a valuable resource for young people struggling to understand the pressing issues of the modern era.

"ALL THINGS ARE POSSIBLE"

On November 4, 2008, in Grant Park in Chicago, Illinois, hundreds of thousands of people stood in the chilly night air. Millions more clustered around their television sets. All were about to witness an American first. A person of color—a black man—had been elected president of the United States, and he was about to give his victory speech. Supporters of Barack Hussein Obama reveled in the celebration. Music filled the night, and peopled danced. And in the evening's most anticipated moment, President-Elect Obama, his wife, Michelle, and their two young daughters arrived onstage. Obama spoke of America's promise and its fulfillment. He said, "If there is anyone out there who still doubts that America is a place where all things are possible, who still wonders if the dream of our founders is alive in our time, who still questions the power of our democracy, tonight is your answer."[1]

Although his remarks hinted at a moment of transformation in American politics, Obama did not mention what was obvious to all: A racial barrier had fallen. The night marked a racial turning point in the history of the United States of America. For the millions of people watching, Obama was not simply a man assuming an office; he was the living embodiment of racial progress.

With Obama's election, the country's painful history of slavery, discrimination, and racism had added a new chapter. The promise of justice and equality for all had found some measure of fulfillment after hundreds of years. While millions of Americans celebrated the victory, politicians and pundits around the world wondered how Obama's victory would change the United States, the most powerful nation on the face of the earth. How could racism continue to exist, many wondered, after a black man had been elected to the presidency? Speaking in India a week after Obama's election, Nobel Prize–winning South African writer Nadine Gordimer made a bold pronouncement: "He is half white and half black. To me, that symbolically represents a kind of advance in recognizing the human tribe as one. In other words, it's bringing together in his own DNA, his blood, what we all wish to see, the end of racism."[2]

Obama's election had provided Gordimer and others throughout the world with optimism that racism might finally be conquered. This sentiment was further echoed in October 2009 when Obama was awarded the Nobel Peace Prize. In office less than a year, Obama himself appeared surprised by the

A man weeps in joy during a celebration in honor of Barack Obama's election. Obama's election to the U.S. presidency marked a turning point in the country, illustrating racial progress, and making many people optimistic about the future of racial equality.

award. But the Nobel committee explained its decision in a statement: "Only very rarely has a person to the same extent as Obama captured the world's attention and given its people hope for a better future."[3]

Racism Is Still Present

Despite the feelings of hope surrounding Obama's historic election and the excitement over his Nobel Prize, racism still exists in the United States and around the world. For example, Obama had unprecedented security long before Election Day. No candidate for president had received protection so early in a campaign before. In the early days of Obama's campaign, Secret Service agents, charged with guarding the president and presidential candidates, investigated death threats, many of them mentioning his race, on an almost daily basis. After Obama's inauguration in January 2009, death threats against him soared, with the Secret Service fielding at least thirty each day. The overwhelming number of threats—much higher than those against any other president—stretched the Secret Service to the breaking point, as agents were often told to work longer hours to handle the increased workload.

Molefi Kete Asante is a professor of African American studies at Temple University in Philadelphia, Pennsylvania. In his book *Erasing Racism*, Asante explains that the nation's long history of oppressing blacks through slavery and racist policies have made racism a difficult issue to deal with. He writes, "The fact is, we cannot dispense with 250 years of involuntary servitude and sweep it under the rug. We cannot dispense with nearly one hundred years of official segregation."[4] Asante adds that "the lingering effects of the enslavement are current and immediate in almost all sectors of American life: health, education, employment, housing, and law."[5]

One of the most glaring examples of continuing racial inequality in America today is the number of young black males in prison compared to the number of whites. Although blacks account for only 13 percent of the U.S. population, they make up 52 percent of the prison population. In fact, one in ten black men in their twenties and early thirties are in prison. These statistics point out a huge difference in the way blacks and whites are treated by the judicial system, as two African American scholars explain:

> Although no longer inscribed in law, [racism] is implicit to processes of law enforcement, prosecution, and incarceration, guiding the behavior of police, prosecutors, judges, juries, wardens, and parole boards. Hence, African Americans continue to experience higher rates of incarceration than do whites charged with similar crimes, endure longer sentences for the same classes of crimes perpetrated by whites, and, compared to white inmates, receive far less consideration by parole boards when being considered for release.[6]

Such differences in the way blacks and whites are treated suggests that the United States and many other nations around the world still have a long way to go in eliminating racial prejudice. In the twenty-first century, racism is very much alive, threatening people's livelihoods, relationships, and their daily lives. In many ways, equality between the races remains an unsatisfied goal.

RACISM TODAY

Racism is the belief that one race is better than another. Racism involves prejudice, or negative opinions, judgments, and attitudes about people based on their race. David Wellman, author of *Portraits of White Racism*, explains that racism is more than just bias against a group of people based on skin color. Rather, Wellman defines racism as a "system of advantage based on race."[7] In other words, racism involves not only discriminating against one race but also upholding the advantages the other race enjoys, including better opportunities for education, housing, and employment.

Racism has been a part of the United States since the earliest days of the nation's history. The first blacks in North America arrived as slaves serving white masters. Slavery existed in the United States for more than 250 years. And although the institution of slavery ended after the Civil War when the Thirteenth Amendment was ratified in 1865, African Americans continued to endure racial oppression at the hands of whites for another century. Not until the Civil Rights Act of 1964 were all forms of legalized racial discrimination finally abolished.

Racism exists in other countries, as well. Stories of the effects of racism—whether it takes an overt or a more subtle form—can be found all over the world. Despite enormous progress that has made life more bearable for people who have historically been oppressed, twenty-first-century racism looks much like its twentieth-century counterpart. Each year, hundreds of thousands of people are discriminated against because of the color of their skin. Thousands of others are harassed, beaten, or even murdered.

Hate in the United States

Racism is often violent. Acts of violence or vandalism against a person because of his or her race, ethnicity, religion, or sexual orientation are called hate crimes, and thousands of people are victims each year. In the United States 7,783 hate crimes were reported in 2008, an increase of 2 percent over the previous year. Police determined that 4,934 of these hate crimes were

An 1829 poster announces an upcoming sale of slaves, along with other "goods" like rice and ribbons. The United Stages engaged in slavery for more than 250 years.

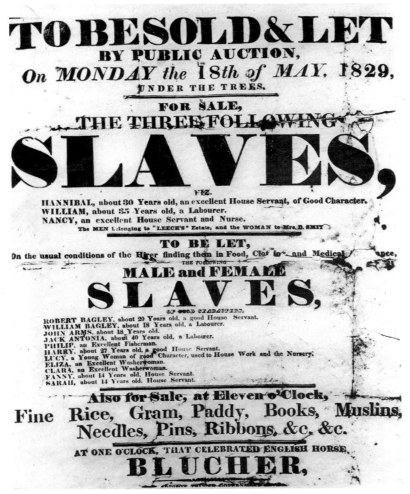

racially motivated, and of these, 72 percent were committed against black people. Hate crimes are not committed against blacks only, however. According to the Southern Poverty Law Center (SPLC), which tracks such crimes, eight blacks, three Jews, three homosexuals, and one Latino become the victims of hate crimes everyday.

Yet blacks remain a primary target for hate crimes. In December 2009, for example, vandals spray painted racial epithets, or insults, on City Hall in Columbia, South Carolina, in response to the candidacies of two black people for mayor. That same month in Queens, New York, a black man was taunted and beaten by a Hispanic man who told him that he did not belong in the neighborhood. Also in December 2009, an African American church in La Porte, Indiana, had a window broken and racial slurs written on its front door.

Hate crimes are not usually crimes committed by one person, acting alone. Some perpetrators identify themselves as members of an organized group. The SPLC identified 926 active hate groups in the United States in 2008, a 50 percent increase since 2000. California has eighty-four such organizations —the highest in the nation. Although not all of these groups are known to be violent, sociologists argue that their very presence can spark acts of racism.

One such hate group is the Arkansas-based White Revolution. This militant white-supremacist group, run by a former high school history teacher, is proud of its racist ideology. On its Web site, the group promises that "the United States of America was born in bloody revolution, and the multiracial cesspool of squabbling minorities squealing for their slice of the affirmative-action pie and taxpayer provided benefits that it has become will die that way."[8] Such extreme language is not uncommon for hate groups attempting to encourage hatred in order to attract new members.

Hate Around the World

While thousands of racially motivated crimes are committed in the United States each year, Europe, Asia, Africa, South America, and the Middle East are not immune to the phenomenon.

Finland, Ireland, China, Greece, Sweden, Denmark, Germany, Spain, and France are but a few of the countries where this kind of violence has risen. The 2007 European Crime and Safety Survey states that government monitoring of racially motivated violence in Finland, Ireland, Sweden, and the United Kingdom, among other countries, indicates that immigrants from Africa are the most common victims of hate crimes in Europe.

On average, 9.9 percent of immigrants to Europe reported that they or members of their families had been targeted, often because of their race. This led some experts to conclude that racism is a motivating factor in these violent acts. Others suggest that such reports may be understated, as many hate crimes go unreported. In addition, in some places overt forms of racism may actually be quietly tolerated by locals.

In Europe and South America particularly, rabid soccer fans regularly flaunt their racist tendencies. Amid the cheers and boos typical of any sporting event, extreme fans known as hooligans frequently shout racial insults, throw garbage, and make monkey noises at black players—insinuating that people of color resemble monkeys. "I think it's unacceptable to behave like that in a football stadium but also in any other walk of life," said María Jesús San Segundo, Spain's education and science minister from 2004 to 2006. "It shows a lack of education. . . . Young people have to realise that regardless of sex, colour or culture every human being is the same."[9]

Many of the fans consider the behavior little more than a show of enthusiasm for their own team. "The kids' chanting last night was stupid but harmless," said Alejandro, a Spanish football fan, after one such event. "Football is always about insulting the other team. The racism wasn't meant seriously."[10]

Alejandro's opinion was echoed by his friend, Miguel, who said, "We Spaniards aren't more racist than any other country. Italy has problems with football and racism, doesn't it? It's much worse than here."[11]

Italy has a population of 60 million people, and 4 million are legal immigrants. However, millions of immigrants reside there illegally. Italy depends on illegal immigrants, who are mostly from West Africa, to work long hours for very little pay

Soccer fans in Argentina wave flags with a swastika during a match. Extreme fans often shout racial insults and engage in other offensive behavior.

picking fruit, a job many Italians consider beneath them. In January 2010 some of the country's worst race riots in years erupted after a legal worker from the African nation of Togo was shot and wounded with a pellet gun in the southern region of Calabria. Other African immigrants, who blamed racism for the attack, took to the streets in protest, throwing rocks, setting cars on fire, and clashing with local police. More than fifty immigrants and police officers were wounded in the two days of rioting that engulfed the entire city of Rosario.

The incident revealed the ugly reality of Italy's dependence on cheap labor and the racism that is often involved. "This event pulled the lid off something that we who work in the sector know well but no one talks about: That many Italian economic realities are based on the exploitation of low-cost foreign labor, living in subhuman conditions, without human rights,"[12] says Flavio di Giacomo, spokesperson for the International Organization for Migration.

Discrimination in the Workplace

Racism is not always expressed through violent actions. Racial discrimination, although typically illegal, remains common in many countries, and the United States is no exception. In 2007 alone, thirty thousand cases of racial discrimination in the workplace were filed with the U.S. Equal Employment Opportunity Commission, which is responsible for enforcing federal laws against discrimination.

Racial discrimination occurs in the workplace when a person is prevented from holding a certain job or from advancing in his or her career because of his or her race. Discriminatory practices in the workplace are reflected in the income disparity between blacks and whites in the United States. According to data from the U.S. Census Bureau, blacks earn on average only 64 percent of what whites earn. Furthermore, 22 percent of blacks live in poverty, whereas only 9 percent of whites do.

Although companies often strive for diversity, minorities rarely fill leadership roles in the United States. A 2007 study by the Executive Leadership Council showed that although blacks held 460 of the 2,000 positions within four steps of chief executive at Fortune 500 companies, less than 1 percent of chief executive officers at Fortune 500 companies are black. David A. Thomas, a professor at Harvard Business School, puts it bluntly: "People of color who start at the same time as an equivalent white person have less of a chance of being at the top echelon [level] in 20 years, in whatever field you're talking about."[13]

And while minority athletes long ago broke down the barriers that kept them from playing sports, few of them hold positions of authority off the field. In 2010, 92.5 percent of university

Jackie Robinson was the first African American to break into major league baseball. In spite of his breakthrough, there is still discrimination in sports programs across the country.

presidents with top-ranked sports programs were white, as were 87.5 percent of athletic directors. The Massachusetts Institute of Technology (MIT), one of the most highly esteemed educational institutions in the United States, recently conducted a study regarding its own recruiting and hiring practices. The study, authored by the Initiative on Faculty Race and Diversity, found that MIT's recruiting efforts resulted in a faculty that was 6 percent black and Hispanic. And those few minority instructors reported an overall dissatisfaction with their experiences at MIT.

EEOC's 2007 Employment Summary by Job Category

Male

Job Categories	White	Black	Hispanic	Asian	Indian
Officials/Admin	201,094	21,992	13,393	5,734	1,052
Professionals	533,645	78,049	52,832	40,921	4,010
Technicians	213,263	33,040	28,473	11,021	1,866
Protective Service	743,459	139,655	112,242	17,131	6,118
Para-Professionals	64,166	25,820	12,602	3,897	656
Admin Support	81,804	23,758	19,900	7,846	1,284
Skilled Craft	305,994	63,283	44,277	9,224	3,501
Service/Maintenance	253,879	122,964	66,561	9,834	3,096

Female

Job Categories	White	Black	Hispanic	Asian	Indian
Officials/Admin	115,247	23,547	10,093	3,914	770
Professionals	614,431	170,546	80,231	51,815	6,188
Technicians	126,582	43,436	25,628	11,073	1,455
Protective Service	132,327	82,481	29,697	3,058	1,975
Para-Professionals	162,278	83,265	35,075	7,665	2,140
Admin Support	527,989	162,446	108,757	24,001	5,651
Skilled Craft	14,378	6,299	1,914	456	220
Service/Maintenance	65,429	57,443	18,910	3,555	1,087

Taken from: U.S. Equal Employment Opportunity Commission, www.eeoc.gov/eeoc/statistics/employment/
jobpat-eeo4/2007/index.cfm.

Whether these employment trends will continue in the future is difficult to gauge, but without minority leadership, many envision a bleak future in which racism and oppression will surely persist. "The biggest challenge is really not having the role models, not seeing yourself, at the senior levels early in your career,"[14] says Clarence Otis Jr., chief executive officer of the Darden Corporation.

RACE AND THE PRESIDENCY

"I think an overwhelming portion of the intensely demonstrated animosity toward President Barack Obama is based on the fact that he is a black man, that he's African American."—Jimmy Carter, thirty-ninth president of the United States.

Quoted in Ewen MacAskill, "Jimmy Carter: Animosity Towards Barack Obama Is Due to Racism," *Guardian*, September 16, 2009, www.guardian.co.uk/world/2009/sep/16/jimmy-carter-racism-barack-obama.

Racial discrimination also occurs early in the employment process, as a 2003 study shows. Researchers Marianne Bertrand of the University of Chicago and Dean Karlan of Yale University sent out nearly five thousand fictional résumés in Boston, Massachusetts, and Chicago, Illinois. Their résumés included some with "white-sounding" names, such as Emily and Greg, and some with "black-sounding" names, such as Lakisha and Jamal. Bertrand and Karlan discovered that the résumés with white-sounding names received 50 percent more calls for interviews than those with black-sounding names, indicating a racial prejudice in hiring practices.

Blacks who do get hired may be subjected to unfair practices in the workplace. One example of this can be found in the class action lawsuit against New York City's Parks and Recreation Department. For years blacks and other minorities who worked in the department rarely received pay raises comparable with their white counterparts and were typically turned down for promotions. Banding together, the employees sued

Students protest at Columbia University in October 2007 after a hangman's noose was placed on an African American professor's office door.

the city, and after nine years, they won their court battle in 2008. The settlement awarded the workers $21 million, much of it in back pay, and the department agreed to change its policies and procedures to ensure fairness in the future. According to the plaintiffs' attorney, Cynthia Rolling, "this case and this settlement should provide inspiration to all employees subjected to unfair and discriminatory treatment on their jobs."[15]

Racism in School

The workplace is only one arena in which racism and prejudice frequently appear. In schools, especially, various forms of racism and racial insensitivity challenge teachers and students around the world on a regular basis. In British schools, for example, forty thousand race-related incidents are reported each year. In 2007, 4,410 students were suspended or expelled for racist behavior, which ranged from racial jokes to the mistreatment of minority teachers. British schools continue to take a hard disciplinary line against activities they deem racially motivated.

In the United States, too, race continues to be a factor in schools. Only about 56 percent of blacks graduate from high school nationwide, compared to 80 percent of whites. Sociologists are reluctant to identify racism as the sole cause for this lack of achievement, but it may be one key factor. Tensions, or even violence, between students of different races often convince young blacks that school just isn't worth attending. And in many cities, crumbling buildings, outdated textbooks, and incompetent staff further discourage students. Each year, broken schools and student financial pressures force thousands of African Americans into the workforce before completing their high school education.

Those that do graduate and attend college likewise find it difficult to finish their degree. According to the *Journal of Blacks in Higher Education*, the nationwide college graduation rate for blacks who attend college is only 43 percent, 20 percent lower than that for whites. The U.S. Census Bureau reports that while 30 percent of whites earn college degrees, only 13 percent of blacks do.

Racial Insensitivity

Racism exists in many forms. Sometimes it is very obvious, as with racially motivated hate crimes, and sometimes it is more subtle, such as when a child makes a racially insensitive comment. But no matter the form racism takes, it is always damaging. Many blacks grow up feeling inferior, as if they do not belong in a "white" world. Racist messages can affect people from a very early age, as an episode in Huntingdon Valley, Pennsylvania, illustrates. In the summer of 2009, a group of mostly African American and Hispanic children from Creative Steps summer camp traveled to the Valley Club to go swimming. Creative Steps had paid $1,950 for the privilege of swimming at the club one day a week during the summer, but the first visit would be the last.

Soon after arriving, fourteen-year-old camper Dymir Baylor heard other pool patrons making racially insensitive comments. He was shocked. He recalled, "I heard a white lady say, 'What are all these black kids doing here? They might do something to

"Never Thought It Would Happen in 2007"

In the fall of 2006 a black high school student in Jena, Louisiana, asked during an assembly if black students could sit beneath a tree where white students usually sat. The next day two nooses hung from the tree. The white students who hung the nooses were suspended, but soon after, tensions rose when a group of black students assaulted a white student who had been taunting them. The six black students involved were immediately arrested, expelled, and charged with attempted murder. One of them, sixteen-year-old Mychal Bell, was charged as an adult. Found guilty by an all-white jury in 2007, Bell's conviction was later overturned. He eventually pleaded guilty to second-degree battery in a plea agreement. Two and a half years after the assault, charges were also reduced for the five other students in a plea agreement. They all pleaded guilty to simple battery and paid fines. The case inspired protests against the school district, rallies in front of the courthouse, and marches in support of Bell and his friends. For many, the incident was a bitter reminder of racial injustice of the past. "The case plays to the fears of many blacks," said civil rights activist Al Sharpton. "You hear the stories from your parents and grandparents, but you never thought it would happen in 2007. I think what resonates in the black community is that this is so mindful of pre-1960 America."

Quoted in Marisol Bello, "La. Beating Case Stirs Racial Anger," *USA Today*, September 7, 2007, www.usatoday

People hold signs and walk in protest of the arrest of six black students in Jena, Louisiana, after they responded violently to a "prank" by white students who hung nooses from trees.

my child.'"[16] Baylor reported the incident to the summer camp's executive director, Alethea Wright.

The children continued playing in the pool for another hour. Later that day Wright approached club president John Duesler about the issue; Duesler was apologetic, she said. But a few days later, Duesler refunded the camp's $1,950; the children from Creative Steps were no longer welcome at the Valley Club. While the club initially refused to comment on the incident, it eventually responded to accusations of racism. "There was concern that a lot of kids would change the complexion . . . and the atmosphere of the club,"[17] said Duesler. A few weeks later, another of the club's leaders defended the club by claiming that the organization's racial makeup was diverse and that the club does not discriminate.

Hidden Bias

Sometimes racism can be so subtle that a person may not even be aware of his or her own prejudices. Yet in most spheres of American life, race remains a powerful, if often unspoken, fact of life.

A 2009 study of racial attitudes in the United States found that even those people who view themselves as non-racist and tolerant may hold unconscious racial prejudices. Researchers divided 120 non-black participants into two groups: "experiencers" and "forecasters." The "experiencers" were placed in a room with a white person and a black person, both part of the study team. A prearranged scenario was played out in which the black person bumped the white person's knee when leaving the room. The white team member would then do one of three things: make no comment, make a moderately racist comment, or make a blatant and vulgar racist comment. In many cases the experiencer added an insulting comment of his or her own. But in all three scenarios, the experiencers reported very little distress over what they had witnessed.

The forecasters, on the other hand, were merely asked to predict their response to each of the three scenarios described above. In both the moderate and extreme scenarios, the forecasters reported they would feel a great deal of distress—much more distress than the experiencers reported actually feeling.

The results of this study surprised the researchers. Psychology professor Kerry Kawakami, the lead researcher, explains, "Some people might think that they're very egalitarian and they don't have to deal with their prejudices, and that it's not related to them at all, when in actual fact they may hold these hidden biases." He added, "This study . . . suggests that there are still really a lot of negative associations with blacks. People are willing to tolerate racism and not stand up against it."[18]

CRIMINAL DIVERSION

"Focusing first and foremost, or worse, solely upon such characteristics . . . as race, ethnicity, national origin or religion in deciding whom to investigate, arrest, and prosecute . . . diverts attention from actual criminal behavior and from the actual perpetrator of a crime."—Timothy K. Lewis, federal judge.

Quoted in Jim Lobe, "Racial Profiling Both Wrong and Counter-Productive, Says Amnesty," CommonDreams.org, September 14, 2004, www.commondreams.org/headlines04/0914-03.htm.

Part of the reason racism is tolerated may be that whites deny it still exists. In January 2008 a survey found that 72 percent of white people believed that blacks overestimated the amount of discrimination against them. Conversely, 82 percent of black people thought that whites underestimated discrimination against blacks. At the very least these statistics show a deep division in how the races perceive one another. Whites, the numbers imply, believe people of color are too sensitive to racial slights. But as Molefi Kete Asante explains in *Erasing Racism*, racial discrimination persists in our nation in both overt and subtle ways. Asante writes,

We [African Americans] walk into an automobile showroom and we are quoted higher prices than whites; we work as cooks in restaurants where whites with less skill and less time in the job are paid more; we step into employment agencies and they direct us away from jobs, high

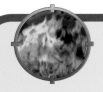

Racism and Health

A variety of scientific studies link race and health. One 2004 study by the *American Journal of Public Health* found that between 1991 and 2000, 886,000 African Americans died because they did not receive the same quality of health care as whites. Lack of insurance, poor service, and a reluctance to trust medical professionals due to historic mistreatment were cited as major factors. For decades statistics showed poorer African Americans living shorter and sicker lives. Then a 2009 study published in the *Journal of the National Cancer Institute* shocked and puzzled the medical community. It revealed that while finances and quality of treatment often degraded the wellness of African Americans, when quality of care was equal to that of whites, blacks remain more vulnerable to certain diseases.

African Americans are 49 percent more likely than whites to die from breast cancer, 61 percent more likely to die from advanced ovarian cancer, and 21 percent more likely to die from advanced prostate cancer. The researchers concluded that biological differences accounted for the discrepancies. Yet some scientists reject the study's findings and are concerned that they could reinforce old racial prejudices. "When I hear scientists talking about racial differences, I worry that it starts to harken back to arguments about genetic inferiority," says Otis W. Brawley, chief medical officer of the American Cancer Society.

Quoted in Rob Stein, "Blacks with Equal Care Still More Likely to Die of Some Cancers," *Washington Post*, July 8, 2009. www.washingtonpost.com/wp-dyn/content/article/2009/07/07/AR2009070702252.html.

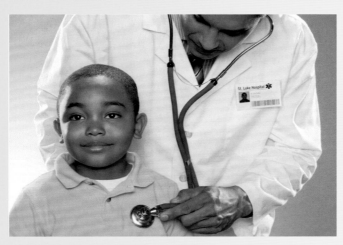

Scientific studies have shown that African Americans do not receive the same quality of health care as whites.

school counselors direct us away from African American Studies courses where we can learn about our history and culture. We are told that there are no apartments available, but when our white friends call the same agency they are told there are several apartments available.[19]

Examples of racism such as these abound in the United States today. William J. Wilson, a professor of sociology at Harvard University, says that he has often experienced a very subtle form of racial prejudice from his white neighbors. He says that in his upper-class neighborhood, whites hesitate to interact with him unless he is wearing business attire. He explains,

> I am an internationally known Harvard professor, yet a number of unforgettable experiences remind me that, as a black male in America looking considerably younger than my age, I am also feared. For example, several times over the years, I have stepped into the elevator of my condominium dressed in casual clothes and could immediately tell from the body language of the other residents in the elevator that I made them feel uncomfortable. Were they thinking, "What is this black man doing in this expensive condominium? Are we in any danger?" . . . When I am dressed casually, I am always a little relieved to step into an empty elevator.[20]

As incidents such as Wilson's encounters in the elevator indicate, racism today looks different than it did fifty or even twenty years ago. The overt discrimination that often accompanied the racism of the past has receded. But other, less obvious forms remain.

WHAT MOTIVATES RACISM?

The causes of racism are wide-ranging and complex. Because people often feel uncomfortable talking about race and ethnicity, the motivations behind racist behavior are often difficult to determine. In addition, many whites are often unaware of racist ideas they may hold. Yet common threads appear to connect incidents of racism. In some cases a belief that one race is better than another can lead to deep-seated prejudice. Sometimes inaccurate assumptions about members of another race can lead to interactions between blacks and whites that are filled with subtle racist undertones. At other times mistrust, misunderstanding, and economic concerns may prompt an instance of racial intolerance.

Fear of the "Other"

Racism begins with the idea that humans can be separated into different groups based on perceived physical differences, such as skin color, facial features, and hair texture. These differences are the basis for what is commonly thought of as "race." Long ago, people believed that blacks and whites were genetically different from one another. Today, however, with advances in human genetics, scientists now know that the two races are not biologically separate. In fact, human beings, no matter where they are from or what their perceived race is, are quite similar in their genetic makeup. Race is merely a social concept, one that people around the world continue to use in order to define how they view and treat one another.

Yet people continue to separate others into distinct "races" and form ideas and opinions about what each race is like. This is due in part to the human tendency to form stereotypes—oversimplified

A nineteenth-century German anthropologist divided humanity into five separate "races," depicted here: Caucasian, center; clockwise from top right: Mongolian, Malayan, Ethiopian, and American Indian. People today still separate others into such categories, which may lead to negative stereotypes.

ways of categorizing other people. The need for a way to put various people into general groups most likely arose in the earliest days of human existence, when knowing which group, family, or tribe one belonged to was necessary for survival. Stereotypes may provide people with a shorthand way to categorize others, but they can be very harmful. They can lead to the belief that because certain people are classified as a group, then they must all be alike. This is especially harmful when a stereotype involves negative traits being associated with the group. For example, various groups of people throughout history have been viewed as dishonest, lazy, stupid, violent, and a host of other negative attributes. The belief that whole groups of people hold undesirable traits can lead to racial prejudice—an unfavorable judgment about other people based on the color of their skin.

FEARING DIVERSITY

"I'm a biological racist. I'd rather have the entire species become extinct except for one white boy and one white girl who were raised by a pack of wild wolves, than have our race go under and the world inherited by Asians and mulattos who can play the classical violin and recite Shakespeare all day long."—Billy Roper, founder of White Revolution, a white supremacist organization.

Quoted in Anti-Defamation League, "White Revolution/Billy Roper," Anti-Defamation League, www.adl.org/Learn/ext_us/w_revolution.asp?LEARN_Cat=Extremism&LEARN _SubCat=Extremism_in_America&xpicked=2&item=WR_BR.

Stereotypes and racial prejudice can lead to a mistrust of people from another racial group. Psychologist Beverly Daniel Tatum explains that racism can begin in childhood and stem from a lack of experience with anyone who is different from oneself. In her book, *"Why Are All the Black Kids Sitting Together in the Cafeteria?" and Other Conversations About Race*, Tatum writes,

The impact of racism begins early. Even in our preschool years, we are exposed to misinformation about people different from ourselves. Many of us grew up in neighborhoods where we had limited opportunities to interact with people different from our own families. When I ask my college students, "How many of you grew up in neighborhoods where most of the people were from the same racial group as your own?" almost every hand goes up. There is still a great deal of social segregation in our communities. Consequently, most of the early information we receive about "others"—people racially, religiously, or socioeconomically different from ourselves —does not come as the result of firsthand experience. The secondhand information we do receive has often been distorted, shaped by cultural stereotypes, and left incomplete.[21]

Origins of Racism

The concept of race is relatively new. The ancient Greeks identified peoples of the world not by skin color or ethnicity but by their actions, dividing them into the categories of "civilized" or "barbarous." Scientists theorize that around 1750 B.C., a light-skinned group now known as Indo-Aryans migrated from Central Asia to India and before long drew a racist distinction between themselves and darker-skinned native peoples. During the Middle Ages, the Arab Empire initially recognized the equality of all races, but in time, as the empire expanded and slave trading became common, negative feelings toward darker-skinned people developed. Arab fathers typically rejected intermarriage between their daughters and black men because darker skin be-came synonymous with strangeness and inferiority. Beginning in the sixteenth century, the slave trade in Europe and the Americas likewise forged deep divisions between races. Generations of black people were owned by whites in the United States until 1865, when slavery was abolished. But American laws and racial prejudice among the general population imposed other kinds of chains: African Americans were segregated, or separated, from whites in neighborhoods, schools, restaurants, and theaters. Nearly one hundred years passed before the fight for civil rights in the 1960s accorded blacks some semblance of equality, but deep-seated racism persisted as many whites fought to maintain their privileged status.

The American Psychological Association (APA) says that it is human nature for people to avoid things that make them feel anxious or uncomfortable. This avoidance contributes to many people's lack of experience with people of another race. The APA explains,

> Our stereotypes of other groups . . . often lead to feelings of anxiety when we encounter the members of [that] group. One of the oldest insights of psychology is that a main way we deal with anxiety is through avoidance: We simply avoid contact with individuals by crossing the street, turning our heads, talking to someone else, hiring someone else for a job, striking up friendships with some-one else we feel more comfortable with, sitting down at the lunch table with those who seem to be more like us.[22]

Such misinformation and lack of contact can reinforce negative stereotypes and lead to inaccurate assumptions about anyone who is a different race. These assumptions may then lead to fear that somehow a person's life will be negatively impacted by a racial group. This fear and mistrust of others goes hand in hand with prejudice and can lead to a person developing negative and hostile attitudes toward others based solely on their race. Such attitudes can also lead to a belief that one race is inherently "better" than another.

A Sense of Superiority

Racial prejudice often develops from one race's sense of superiority over another. In the early United States the belief that blacks were an inferior race was the cornerstone of slavery. Even after slavery ended, generations of prejudice against blacks encouraged whites to view themselves as better than African Americans. Black people had little political or cultural power. They were typically relegated to second-class status and had no access to the kinds of education available to most whites. Only in the mid–twentieth century did blacks begin to gain equal rights with whites in the United States. But in many ways, a subtle attitude of white superiority still exists in the country, even though it may often be at an unconscious level.

This sign from the mid-twentieth century in America designates a "white only" waiting room. Prejudice against one race is often the result of a sense of superiority over those who are different.

Part of the reason this attitude of white superiority continues to exist is that it allows whites to feel good about their own identity and that of their group. Being part of the dominant group in a society—or the "in" group—can lead some people to believe that they actually are superior in some way to members of the "out" group. In addition, members of the "in" group enjoy certain benefits and advantages. The APA explains why prejudices and stereotypes that confer privilege to one group over another often remain unexamined:

Because stereotypes may help us feel better about ourselves, we avoid challenging these stereotypes. In other words, we become defensive and protective of our worldviews and only reluctantly question our deepest assumptions. And these worldviews help protect not only our self-esteem, but also real-world privileges and benefits that accrue to us as members of an in group. For example, racist discrimination by banks that hurts African American communities by limiting mortgages to these areas also benefits White neighborhoods by making more money available to them. . . . So, maintaining our prejudiced views of others allows us to feel better about our own group and to avoid challenging unfair social practices that benefit us.[23]

When these negative racist ideas and prejudicial attitudes remain intact, it enables whites to maintain the power and advantages they hold in society. This is sometimes referred to as "white privilege." Some people—for example, members of white supremacy groups—are very aware of their desire to keep white privilege intact. But others may never have stopped to think about the fact that they enjoy certain advantages simply because they are white. Yet whether people acknowledge it or not, white superiority remains a factor in interactions between blacks and whites today.

Racial Profiling

Racial profiling is a method of using racial or ethnic characteristics to determine whether a person is likely to commit a crime. Law enforcement agencies around the world have relied on racial profiling for centuries to predict who will or will not commit a crime. For example, since the terrorist attacks on the United States in September 2001, fears of more attacks have led to greater security screening of Arabs, who are stopped, searched, and sometimes barred from boarding airplanes. Millions of minorities believe that racial profiling targets them on a daily basis. Security officials charged with protecting citizens argue that these tactics are necessary, but critics say it is unfair and actually leads to further racial prejudice because racial profiling reinforces the negative stereotype of blacks and other minorities as untrustworthy and contributes to such attitudes permeating society.

Racial profiling of African American drivers is so common in the United States that it has come to be called DWB, or "Driving While Black."

According to 2008 statistics, 32 million Americans claim to have been racially profiled. Most of them are African American, Hispanic, or Arab. The racial profiling of black drivers has become so common in the United States that African Americans have invented a phrase and an acronym to describe it. "Driving While Black," or DWB, may be a symptom of deep-seated racial prejudice. The prevalence of the phenomenon itself may also contribute to negative societal perceptions of blacks.

LEARNING TO HATE

"Racism is learned behavior. The way in which a white child behaves toward an ethnic group is a direct reflection of their parents' attitude about race. If a child hears his or her parents vocalizing racial stereotypes, the child learns to identify everyone in that group by those labels."—Shar'Ron Maxx Mahaffey, author.

Shar'Ron Maxx Mahaffey, "Is Racism Taught or Learned?" Helium, www.helium.com/items/882142-is-racism-taught-or-learned.

Numerous African Americans who have been pulled over, questioned, and even searched by police believe they were targeted for no other reason than their race. This list includes actors Wesley Snipes, Will Smith, LeVar Burton, and Blair Underwood, as well as athletes Marcus Allen, Al Joyner, and Edwin Moses. High-profile attorney Johnnie Cochran was stopped by police, too, when he was an assistant district attorney in Los Angeles, California. He had his two young children in the backseat of his car when he was stopped by police. Cochran says that when he looked in the rearview mirror, "the police were out of their car with their guns out." The police accused Cochran of driving a stolen vehicle and began to search the car. The police found no evidence that the car was stolen and let Cochran go, but the incident left a lasting mark on Cochran and his children. Cochran explains, "[The officers] had their guns out and my kids were in that car crying. My daughter said, 'Daddy, I thought you were with the police.' I had to explain to her why this happened."[24]

Many other blacks in the United States say they have had a similar experience: They have been pulled over by police who use the traffic stop as an excuse to search them and their cars. But racial profiling is not limited to traffic stops. In some cases, racial profiling can take place in businesses, schools, and private residences.

A Widely Publicized Incident

Some people think that racial profiling was at least partly to blame for a widely publicized incident in the summer of 2009 between a black man and a white police officer in Massachusetts. Harvard University professor Henry Louis Gates Jr. is a well-known and widely respected African American scholar who has written for a variety of publications. He also hosted the PBS miniseries *African American Lives*, which explored the genealogy of blacks in America.

Gates lives in an upper-middle-class, mostly white neighborhood in Cambridge, Massachusetts. On July 16, 2009, Gates returned to his home in a taxicab after having spent two weeks out of town. Jet-lagged and in need of sleep, Gates tried to open the front door to his house, but it was jammed. After a few more attempts, he and his cab driver got the door open, but by this time a neighbor had called 911, saying she saw unfamiliar men possibly trying to break into the house. She did not identify the color of their skin. However, some people believe that the events that transpired next were affected by very subtle racist attitudes.

Not long after the neighbor called 911, a police car arrived. One of the officers was Sergeant James Crowley, an eleven-year veteran of the Cambridge Police Department and a police academy instructor. Crowley approached the front door and asked Gates to step outside. Gates describes the incident and his reaction to the sergeant's request:

> All of a sudden, there was a policeman on my porch. And I thought, "This is strange." So I went over to the front porch . . . and I said "Officer, can I help you?" And he said, "Would you step outside onto the porch." And the way he said it, I knew he wasn't canvassing for the police

benevolent association. All the hairs stood up on the back of my neck, and I realized that I was in danger. And I said to him no, out of instinct. I said, "No, I will not.". . .

He didn't say, "Excuse me, sir, is there a disturbance here, is this your house?"—he demanded that I step out on the porch, and I don't think he would have done that if I was a white person.[25]

Crowley noted in his police report that Gates's behavior was belligerent. Crowley wrote that when he asked Gates to step outside, Gates said, "Why, because I'm a black man in America?"[26] After Crowley made several requests for Gates's identification, Gates showed Crowley his Harvard University identification. As Crowley turned to leave, Gates apparently followed him, repeatedly asking to see Crowley's identification and badge number. The verbal sparring between the two men continued until Crowley placed Gates in handcuffs and arrested him for disorderly conduct.

As the incident gained international attention, charges of racism swirled around Crowley. For days afterward, scholars and pundits traded views not only on who was at fault but also on what the arrest of an eminent African American scholar said about the state of race relations. Many called it a case of racial profiling. After commenting on the situation and the controversy, President Barack Obama invited both men to the White House. Subsequently, the so-called Beer Summit occurred on July 30. Gates, Crowley, Obama, and Vice President Joe Biden sat at an outdoor table drinking beers and talking.

After the meeting, Obama said that despite the media hoopla surrounding the event, it was all about communicating with one another. "This is . . . having a drink at the end of the day and hopefully giving people an opportunity to listen to each other,"[27] he said.

In a brief news conference following the Beer Summit, Crowley said, "What you had today was two gentlemen who agreed to disagree on a particular issue. We didn't spend too much time dwelling on the past, and we decided to look forward."[28]

Some people question whether Gates's arrest was actually a case of racial profiling at all. At the very least the controversy reminded Americans of the racial sensitivities that remain, despite the progress that has been made on so many fronts.

Race and the Unconscious Mind

Blacks and whites often respond to one another based on attitudes they each hold about the other's race—attitudes they may hold at an unconscious level. In fact, one of the main motivations for racial prejudice may actually be deeply ingrained racist attitudes that people are unaware they hold. Few people would admit to holding a racial bias; fewer still would describe themselves as racists. Yet four leading universities have devised a series of online tests that measure people's tendency toward bias or prejudice, with surprising results.

From left to right: Vice President Joe Biden, Henry Louis Gates, James Crowley, and President Barack Obama talk at the "Beer Summit" in July 2009.

The Ku Klux Klan: A History of Hate

After the American Civil War, the Ku Klux Klan (KKK), from the Greek word *kyklos*, or circle, was founded in the South. The KKK's first recruits vowed to restore and maintain white power at a time when many feared that newly freed African Americans were being given too many rights. Because the KKK believes blacks to be inferior to whites, they attempted to reverse the tide of African American progress. Wearing white sheets and hoods, Klan members terrorized African Americans by nailing threatening messages to the doors of their houses, burning large crosses in their front yards, and even murdering them by lynching. During the late 1800s, laws banning Klan activity were enacted, and many of its leaders were imprisoned. The Klan reemerged in 1915 with the release of the epic film *The Birth of a Nation*. The movie portrays blacks as shiftless and greedy and Klansmen as heroic do-gooders, saving the country from a black takeover. Membership in the new Klan skyrocketed, reaching 6 million by 1924. But the growing civil rights movement soon pushed the KKK to the fringes of society. Today the Klan's numbers have again dwindled, yet it still exists and remains a potent force of hate.

The 1915 film The Birth of a Nation *led to the reemergence of the Ku Klux Klan in the United States.*

The Implicit Association Test (IAT) is designed to measure the speed with which people categorize images they are shown. There are several types of IATs that measure bias in various areas, such as gender or age, but the most common IAT measures racial bias. This form of the IAT asks test takers to quickly categorize faces, black and white, that appear on the computer screen using certain words, such as "evil," "glorious," or "wonderful." Because those taking the test are encouraged to work fast, they give little conscious thought to their answers. What IAT analysts have discovered is that 80 percent of those who take the test show a bias toward white faces. Even 50 percent of black respondents indentified favorably with whites.

Malcolm Gladwell, the son of a white father and a black mother, writes extensively about IATs in his book, *Blink*. After taking the test himself, he felt slightly embarrassed by his own results. Even though he is well educated and multiracial, he, too, discovered he had prejudices he was not even aware of. After taking the test four times, Gladwell was rated as having a "moderate automatic preference for whites." He wondered, "Does this mean I'm a racist, a self-hating black person?"[29] No, he reasoned; it simply meant that attitudes on race are based on both the biases people are aware of and those that are unconscious, or hidden, even from themselves.

Economics and Social Status

A variety of unconscious ideas may be at play in racism. For example, elitist ideas about socioeconomic status may be so ingrained that people may not be fully aware they hold such a prejudice. Many people—black and white—look down on others who have less-prestigious jobs, earn less money, drive less-expensive cars, or live in smaller homes than they do. This can be a powerful motive for racism when so many African Americans live in poverty. In 2008 the poverty rate in the United States rose to 13.2 percent, the highest level in more than a decade. According to the U.S. Census Bureau, 39.8 million Americans live below the poverty level, and 24 percent of them are black. In a nation where social status and material wealth are prized, minorities continue to lag behind whites.

In addition, blacks and other minorities are sometimes blamed for their own predicament. This is known as blaming the victim, and it comes about because humans like to believe the world is fair and just and that bad things only occur to those who deserve it. So, if the world is fair, then those who are in a bad situation must have done something to deserve their misfortune. Along with blaming victims for their own predicament is the idea that if people just tried hard enough, they could make their situation better. These ideas play a part in racist attitudes about blacks being poor because they are lazy or do not care enough about their situation to do something about it. Victim blaming is something that is deeply ingrained in society, and many people may not realize they hold such an attitude.

RACIAL IDENTITY

"To a grave extent people of color who self-segregate are in collusion with the forces of racism . . . they claim they would like to see come to an end. Racism will never end as long as the color of anyone's skin is the foundation of their identity."—bell hooks, cultural critic and social activist.

bell hooks, *Belonging: A Culture of Place*, New York: Taylor & Francis, 2008.

The reasons for racism are varied and complex. Some are centuries old, while others have come about more recently. Many stem from unconscious attitudes that people hold and never think about. However, racism is pervasive throughout society, even at the unconscious level. In multicultural societies, people have little choice but to try and tolerate one another, regardless of racial differences. When common sense does not prevail, however, laws are often necessary to halt the spread of racism and provide equal opportunity for all.

CHAPTER 3

FIGHTING RACISM

In democratic countries the elected government works for the citizenry, representing their views and making laws that reflect the values of the majority of the people. Over time the will of the people evolves, and laws once thought to be fair and just are deemed outdated, even discriminatory.

During the second half of the twentieth century, unprecedented progress was made in the United States to ensure equality for all citizens. Women fought for and won more control over their destinies. Homosexuals demanded equal rights and began to claim victories in achieving them, and minorities of different backgrounds and ethnicities continued their struggle for civil rights. Despite these revolutionary developments, the fight for racial equality and justice remains a work in progress, especially as some efforts to right past wrongs appear to have only made the issue even more complicated.

Affirmative Action

Affirmative action is giving special preference to people because of their race, ethnicity, or gender. The goal of affirmative action is to provide equal opportunity and to encourage—even demand—diversity in the workplace, in schools, in government, and in other arenas. Affirmative action can also be implemented to make amends for past wrongs, such as slavery or other racial injustices.

Affirmative action is controversial in the United States. The Fourteenth Amendment to the U.S. Constitution, which was ratified in 1868, protects all American citizens, regardless of race, gender, or religion, from discrimination. Minorities, however,

President Lyndon Johnson speaks with a Howard University professor in 1965 after a speech at the university in which he discussed the need for affirmative action.

continued to be legally discriminated against for another hundred years. In the mid–twentieth century, white Americans still received preferential treatment over blacks in virtually all areas of life, including hiring practices, job promotions, wages, housing, and university admissions. The lack of access to a quality education made it even harder for blacks to compete against whites in the workplace. The unemployment rate for blacks in the early 1960s was twice that of whites, and black men earned barely more than half of what white men earned. As a consequence, 55 percent of blacks were living in poverty in 1960.

President Lyndon B. Johnson was an outspoken champion of civil rights for African Americans. In 1965 in a speech he delivered at Howard University, a predominantly African American school in Washington, D.C., Johnson explained why he believed that protective measures such as affirmative action were necessary in order to increase equality. He said,

> In far too many ways American Negroes have been another nation: deprived of freedom, crippled by hatred, the doors of opportunity closed to hope. . . .
>
> You do not take a person who, for years, has been hobbled by chains and liberate him, bring him up to the starting line of a race and then say, "you are free to compete with all the others," and still justly believe that you have been completely fair.
>
> Thus it is not enough just to open the gates of opportunity. All our citizens must have the ability to walk through those gates.[30]

In an effort to combat the racial inequality that existed in the United States, Johnson signed the Civil Rights Act of 1964. This act prohibits discrimination on the basis of race or sex in the workplace, public facilities, union membership, and federally funded programs. The act also established the Equal Employment Opportunity Commission (EEOC), which led the way to the use of affirmative action. With affirmative action blacks were to be given preferential treatment in hiring practices and university admissions. Employers were ordered not only to cease discriminating against people of color and other minorities but to actively hire them.

After Johnson left office, subsequent presidents amended affirmative action, and dozens of court cases have either challenged or upheld the government policy. Writing in support of affirmative action in 1978, U.S. Supreme Court justice Harry Blackmun said, "In order to get beyond racism, we must first take account of race. There is no other way. And in order to treat some persons equally, we must treat them differently."[31]

Is Affirmative Action Necessary?

Thanks to affirmative action programs, blacks now found themselves being hired for jobs that formerly were closed to them and admitted to universities that formerly barred them. One notable example is Supreme Court justice Clarence Thomas, who attended Yale Law School in the 1970s through the university's affirmative action program. Any organization that accepts funding from the government is legally required to hire or admit a certain percentage of women, blacks, and other minorities. This requirement, known as the quota system, remains one of the most controversial aspects of affirmative action, and in recent years mandated affirmative action based on race has come under heavy criticism. These critics call affirmative action "reverse discrimination" that unfairly affects white Americans who, despite better qualifications, may not be selected because they are not black or another minority.

Others argue that the United States has changed dramatically since affirmative action was first enacted, and therefore, the race-based policy is no longer necessary. Instead, they believe affirmative action would serve a better purpose if used to help the economically needy, regardless of race. "As this generation rises, race-based discrimination needs to go," *New York Times* columnist Ross Douthat writes. "The explicit scale-tipping in college admissions should give way to class-based affirmative action; the de facto racial preferences required of employers by anti-discrimination law should disappear."[32]

Another vocal opponent of affirmative action is Ward Connerly, a black conservative. To Connerly the best evidence that

A student at Bridgeport University in Connecticut demonstrates in support of affirmative action in 2003. Affirmative action has come under increasing criticism in recent years.

affirmative action is outdated is the rise of President Barack Obama. "The whole argument in favor of race preferences is that there is 'institutional racism'. . . in American life, and you need affirmative action to level the playing field," says Connerly. "How can you say there is institutional racism when people in Nebraska vote for a guy who is a self-identified black man?"[33]

Obama himself appeared to echo this view when asked whether his own daughters should benefit from affirmative action when they attend college. "I think that my daughters should probably be treated by any [college] admissions officer as folks who are pretty advantaged," Obama said. "We should take into account white kids who have been disadvantaged and have grown up in poverty and shown themselves to have what it takes to succeed."[34]

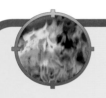

Thurgood Marshall: Civil Rights Pioneer

Thurgood Marshall, the first black justice to serve on the U.S. Supreme Court, was the grandson of a slave. Yet when Marshall was young, his father instilled in him a love of the United States and its laws. After being denied admission to the University of Maryland Law School because he was black, Marshall completed his law degree at Howard University, a traditionally African American institution. There, he was influenced by Charles Hamilton Houston, who encouraged his law students to study the Constitution and demand—through the courts—equal treatment for all people under the law.

After law school, Marshall successfully sued the University of Maryland to admit a young African American in 1933. In dozens of other cases, Marshall chipped away at the legal framework of American racism. Perhaps his greatest victory was *Brown v. Board of Education* in 1954. Marshall successfully argued against segregation in public schools, and with that single case, he helped change the lives of American schoolchildren forever. Marshall was appointed to the Supreme Court in 1967, and he served until 1991 when he retired. He died in 1993.

Glenn C. Loury is an economics professor at Brown University. He sympathizes with the plight of the poor, but he fears that an emphasis on finances might adversely affect the number of African Americans attending college. He explains,

> If we say affirmative action at leading American universities is now open to poor people, regardless of their race, no more of these middle class blacks who have lower test scores getting into places like Princeton or Harvard or any place like that. The result of that . . . will be for every black that might have benefited, there are going to be ten poor whites who could potentially benefit. It will be a significant reduction of the number of blacks at these institutions.[35]

Today the disadvantages faced by many black Americans may have lessened, but how best to legally eradicate racism and racist policies remains open for debate. If racism is no longer an issue, then policies such as affirmative action may be unnecessary. But if race continues to influence which person is hired for a job or admitted to a particular college, then legislators will need to work to keep it alive.

Denial of Racism

Despite all the gains of affirmative action, racial prejudice does still persist in many aspects of daily life for African Americans. Racism in the workplace can be difficult to eliminate entirely, because perceptions of which actions are or are not racist may be different for blacks and whites. Thomas Pettigrew, a professor of social psychology at University of California Santa Cruz, and Joanne Martin, a professor of social psychology at Stanford University, have researched the interactions between whites and blacks in the workplace. They report that a subtle racism still persists in the United States, concluding that whites often are not conscious that certain behaviors or comments are viewed as racist by blacks. Pettigrew and Martin explain,

> Often the black is the only person in a position to draw the conclusion that prejudice is operating in the work situation. . . . Many whites remain unconvinced of the reality of

subtle prejudice and discrimination, and come to think of their black coworkers as "terribly touchy" and "overly sensitive" to the issue. For such reasons, the modern forms of prejudice frequently remain invisible even to its perpetrators.[36]

This racial discrimination in the workplace was experienced by S. Mary Wills, an African American woman who works in human resources. Wills says that both her supervisor and the

President George W. Bush is introduced by NAACP president Bruce Gordon in 2006. The Bush administration pursued fewer civil rights cases than other administrations and came under criticism for lack of enforcement.

director of her department repeatedly made racially insensitive comments. When she complained about the situation, however, she was told she was overreacting. Wills, who has since left the company, explains,

> My former employer specifically used language stating that I had a "fear of being picked on" and they accused me of being "very, very emotional" and "very stressed out." In other words, they were claiming that some sort of school yard or clique-related issue and what they proclaimed to be my personal weaknesses were the causes of the issues at work and not the active racism.[37]

Such denial by whites that racism is occurring in the workplace may be part of the reason that current civil rights laws are not always enforced. This issue took center stage in late 2009 when a report from the U.S. Government Accountability Office suggested that the administration of President George W. Bush pursued fewer civil rights cases than that of his predecessor. President Bush was in office from 2001 to 2008. Between 2001 and 2007, the Civil Rights Division of the Justice Department investigated 324 cases of housing discrimination. During President Bill Clinton's years in office, 1993 to 2000, the Civil Rights Division investigated 676 cases. One possible explanation is that civil rights abuses dramatically declined during the Bush years, but experts doubt this to be the case.

Thomas E. Perez, assistant attorney general of the Civil Rights Division, commented on the lack of civil rights enforcement under the Bush administration. "The division," he says, "was not doing all that it could to fulfill our responsibility to enforce all the civil rights laws fairly and aggressively."[38] Wade Henderson, president of the Leadership Conference on Civil Rights, puts it more bluntly. In "almost every significant area," he says, the Bush administration ignored the reality "of the American experience with race."[39]

Enforcing Current Laws

The reality of the discrimination that many blacks face on the job is often fairly grim. Those who complain that they have been

A Ku Klux Klan member holds a noose, warning African Americans to stay away from voting polls in 1939. The KKK and the noose are symbols of racism in the United States.

subjected to racial prejudice or insensitivity may find that supervisors or coworkers retaliate. Such retaliation can take the form of ridicule and threats, being assigned to perform menial tasks, having pay raises or promotions withheld, and even being fired.

Racial harassment and retaliation were the impetus for a lawsuit filed in October 2009 by the EEOC against Spartan Plumbing, located in Arizona. The EEOC enforces federal laws that prohibit discrimination in the workplace. In its lawsuit, the EEOC states that a black worker at Spartan was repeatedly subjected to harassment based on his race. The worker was given the least desirable tasks to perform on a daily basis. Coworkers and supervisors alike used racial slurs when speaking to and

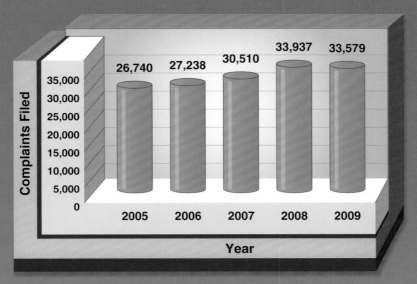

Race-Based Complaints

This bar graph shows the number of complaints filed in the United States alleging race-based discrimination.

Taken from: U.S. Equal Employment Opportunity Commission, www.eeoc.gov/eeoc/statistics/enforcement/race.cfm.

about him. One day in June 2007 the worker found "KKK" written in paint on the floor at his worksite. He also found a noose fashioned out of insulation—a clear symbol of racism because of its association with lynchings of blacks in the past. When the worker complained about this incident to managers at Spartan, he was fired.

When the EEOC investigated the incident, it determined that "this racist misconduct was tolerated in the workplace and the company compounded the problem by firing the victim. This only makes a bad situation worse."[40] Mary Jo O'Neill, regional attorney for the EEOC's Phoenix District Office, says,

> The incidents alleged in this complaint remind us that racism remains a factor in the workplace. Such bold racist actions must be addressed and eradicated by employers in the work environment. The EEOC will continue to vigorously defend the federally protected rights of victims who are subjected to discrimination and who exercise their rights to complain about discrimination to employers.[41]

Fighting Perceptions Around the World

Eliminating racial prejudice in the workplace often involves battling not only overt acts of racism like the ones described in the EEOC lawsuit against Spartan Plumbing, but also perceptions and beliefs regarding race. One of the most prevalent of these perceptions is the widely held, and often unconscious, belief that light skin is better than darker skin. A recent study conducted by scholar Matthew Harrison illustrates this belief. Harrison asked a group of white college students to make hiring recommendations based on a series of fake photographs and résumés. The students preferred light-skinned African American men and women over darker ones. Harrison's analysis determined that such preferences originated during the time of slavery, when light-skinned children of slaves were treated better than their darker counterparts.

Further evidence suggests that for many people throughout the world, "light makes right." For example, in the United States lighter-skinned Latinos make on average five thousand dollars a

A student is photographed as part of the quota program at a Brazilian university. Such policies are intended to provide equal privileges to people of all colors.

year more than darker-skinned Latinos. Statistics show that lighter-skinned politicians are more likely to be elected to office, and darker-skinned people of color often serve longer jail sentences.

Because of the advantages associated with lighter skin, some people have tried various means to prevent their skin from becoming darker, such as wearing protective clothing or staying indoors to avoid the sun. Other people have taken more extreme measures. Each year, millions of dollars are spent on skin-lightening products in the United States and other countries. In late 2009 former Chicago Cubs slugger Sammy Sosa created controversy when he appeared in public with noticeably lighter skin. While Sosa called it skin "rejuvenation," others criticized him and accused him of trying to reject his Dominican heritage by lightening his skin.

THE END OF GLOBAL RACISM

"Each day millions of people experience some form of discrimination solely because of their skin color. . . . After years of failing to engage in this progressive initiative, the US is taking an active role in defending human rights and ending global racism."—Sara Furguson, former Cornell University student.

Sara Furguson, "Fighting Racism," *Cornell Daily Sun*, February 24, 2009, http://cornell sun.com/node/35515.

Harvard scholar and journalist Shankar Vedantam believes this apparent desire for whiter skin is rarely conscious: "This isn't racism, per se: it's colorism, an unconscious prejudice that isn't focused on a single group like blacks so much as on *blackness* itself. Our brains, shaped by culture and history, create intricate caste hierarchies that privilege those who are physically and culturally whiter and punish those who are darker."[42]

The perception that lighter is better is not limited to the United States. In Brazil, for example, people with brown or black skin earn only half of what their lighter-skinned counterparts do. Before 2001 few darker Brazilians were educated at the country's universities. Recent attempts have been made to root out racism in Brazilian society, but old habits are hard to eradicate. According to sociology professor Edward Telles, "most discrimination in Brazil is subtle and includes slights, aggressions and numerous other informal practices, especially . . . racial insults."[43]

Even in particular Brazilian families, lighter-skinned siblings are more likely to stay in school while their darker brothers or sisters drop out. Part of the problem, writes Telles, may be that Brazilians traditionally deny the presence of racism. Yet Brazilian

The End of Legalized Racism in South Africa

In South Africa apartheid was a legal form of racial segregation from 1948 to 1994. It came from laws passed by British colonial rulers in the late nineteenth century. The earliest laws restricted the movement of the black population in order to protect the minority white population, known as Afrikaners. By 1948 restrictions on people of color were tightened when Afrikaners—mostly of northern European heritage—came to power.

Life under apartheid became increasingly more difficult for black South Africans. By the mid-1950s hundreds of thousands of blacks had lost the right to vote. According to the Prohibition of Mixed Marriages Act, the races could not mingle or start a family. Black people had to carry identification cards to pass from one part of the country to another, and employment discrimination based on race was made legal. Eventually, black South Africans were completely stripped of citizenship. By 1990 a crippled economy, decades of racial violence, and worldwide condemnation convinced President F.W. de Klerk to dismantle apartheid. In 1994 South Africa held its first free and multiracial election. Yet despite the end of apartheid, social, political, and economic inequalities between black and white South Africans continue to exist today.

Supporters of Frederik de Klerk gather in South Africa in 1994. De Klerk ended the policy of apartheid that discriminated against and oppressed the black majority in that country.

television and advertising present mostly white faces to viewers and consumers, virtually denying the existence of Brazilians of differing hues. One solution to redress the racial inconsistency is racial quotas, which legally require universities and public institutions to enroll or hire a certain number of nonwhites, regardless of their skills. It remains to be seen whether such policies can succeed where centuries of coexistence between white and nonwhite Brazilians has bred only prejudice and distrust.

Despite the presence of policies designed to ensure equality, such as racial quotas, the fight to overcome racism around the world often boils down to something much more basic. *Kuwait Times* columnist Muna Al-Fuzai believes that combating patterns of racist thinking is often a battle people must wage within themselves. And she decries the racist belief that lighter skin is better. "It is wrong to place one's self esteem on skin color," she writes. "Your destiny was decided when you were born. . . . I love the color of my skin and am proud of myself. I wouldn't want to change it for anything in the world."[44]

Legalized Racism

While many countries have worked to minimize the impact of racism and treat their citizens fairly and with respect in recent decades, a few nations have moved in the opposite direction. In such cases governments have worked to put in place laws that racially discriminate against members of the population. In these instances, attempts to fight racism have backfired and only compounded what was already a difficult problem.

One example of this can be seen in the southern African nation of Zimbabwe, formerly known as Rhodesia. The country is a former British colony, and for decades the British and the minority white population controlled the country, refusing to cede any power to the country's black majority. In 1980 Robert Mugabe led the battle for black rule in the African nation and became prime minister, and later president. In 2000 Mugabe began a policy in which government troops seized land owned by white farmers and redistributed it to black Zimbabweans.

The land policy was heavily criticized worldwide, and Mugabe was labeled a racist for his actions. Yet many view Mugabe's policy as a way of righting a past wrong. Zimbabwe's ugly colonial past, in which white rulers made all laws and stole land that rightfully belonged to blacks, is seen by some Zimbabweans as reason enough to take the land back now, even by force.

The remaining white farmers took their case to a regional tribunal, asking the court to rule Mugabe's policy illegal. In one ruling, judges ordered that the farmers could keep their land, citing it as a clear case of racial discrimination. Mugabe, though, refused to accept the court's decision, and the evictions of white farmers continued.

TARGETING RACISM

"So we must recognise that we will not succeed in tackling racism without tacking all forms of discrimination, prejudice and inequality. We have to redouble our efforts to promote greater equality for all, and combine that with action to target the specific problems faced by particular groups."—John Denham, member of British Parliament.

"John Denham: Tackling Racism Means Tackling All Forms of Discrimination," *Independent*, January 15, 2010, www.independent.co.uk/opinion/commentators/ john-denham-tackling-racism-means-tackling-all-forms-of-discrimination-1868357.html.

In February 2009 Mugabe used the occasion of his eighty-fifth birthday to warn that the country's white farmers had little choice but to give up their land. "Land distribution will continue. It will not stop," Mugabe said. "The few remaining white farmers should quickly vacate their farms as they have no place there."[45]

Charles Lock vowed to fight Mugabe's directive. He is among approximately four hundred white farmers who refused to give up land they believe is rightfully and legally theirs. Like Lock, Ben Freeth steadfastly rejects Mugabe's eviction policies, but life in Zimbabwe gets more difficult by the day. Freeth has been beaten and harassed by squatters living on his farm. "One time they came round with burning sacks at night and they started making a huge noise and ringing a great big bell and shouting and screaming," says Freeth. "They were going underneath

A white farmer assists his workers to harvest tobacco in Zimbabwe. Under President Robert Mugabe, government troops seized land from white farmers and redistributed it to blacks.

the thatch [straw covering on a house] saying we are going to burn your house down if you don't get out."[46]

Incidents such as this are not uncommon in Zimbabwe, where official policy has openly incited racial conflict. As this situation demonstrates, the fight to rectify past wrongs is very complex. It remains a tangled and imperfect process in nations around the world, including the United States. In countries where legalized racism still exists, or where policies favor one racial group over another, it is typically up to average citizens to demand change and fight for their human rights, regardless of the consequences.

PREVENTING RACISM

Many scholars argue that racism can never be completely prevented. The use of race to insult, oppress, or marginalize may be minimized in the years to come but will remain an ever-present facet of human experience. Yet studies have also shown that racism is not an innate, genetically inherited trait. Instead, racial prejudice comes about during socialization—the process of learning about one's social environment. Mothers and fathers, sisters and brothers, teachers and friends, all play a part in building a child's perception of race. Historian Robin D.G. Kelley puts it this way: "[Racism] is not about how you look, it is about how people assign meaning to how you look."[47]

That meaning is conveyed to children early in life. The way children are raised, the schools they attend, and their interactions with people of various backgrounds in the community can all have a profound effect on how they view race. Because of this, experts agree that the most effective way to prevent racism is by eliminating racial bias early in a person's life. However, it is never too late to begin educating people about racism and the effects of prejudice on others. There are numerous programs in place in schools, communities, and businesses that are designed to help raise awareness of racism and increase tolerance for others.

Starting Early

Parents are often a child's first teachers. Children's earliest ideas about the way society works, as well as the ways in which people relate to one another, begin within the family setting. Parents and families typically lay the foundation for children's later attitudes toward others. Because of this, a child's ideas about

An Iraqi child wears an anti-Semitic placard during a demonstration. Children's attitudes toward others are formed in part by parents and family.

people of another race—whether black or white—begin within the home.

The Anti-Racist Alliance Trust, a group in the United Kingdom that works to eliminate racism at all levels of society, states that racism often begins with the ideas and attitudes some parents instill in their children. The group explains that parents are in a unique position to combat racism, and they must be vigilant about challenging racism whenever it appears so that children learn tolerance and respect for others. On its Web site, the group states,

> Parents should teach their child to enjoy, respect, value and appreciate other races and religions from birth—they should not wait until the child is old enough to ask questions or when the child starts mixing with other children because by then they have already got opinions of their own—if the parents don't educate their children about racism, those children will get their education from the TV, from overhearing comments, from the media or the playground.[48]

Experts agree that all parents, whether they are black or white, should discuss race and acceptance of others with their children. Yet a 2007 study published in the *Journal of Marriage and Family* revealed a startling statistic. Of the seventeen thousand families of kindergarten-age children in the study, 75 percent of white parents rarely, if ever, speak about race with their children. The author of a similar study on racist attitudes, Birgitte Vittrup of the Children's Research Lab at the University of Texas, offers one reason why parents may not discuss race openly with their children—many simply do not feel comfortable doing so. When some of the parents dropped out of the study Vittrup was conducting, they told her, "We don't want to have these conversations with our child. We don't want to point out skin color."[49]

Some people may indeed feel that any discussion of race or other characteristics that make another person "different" may be impolite. Further, they may fear that discussing race with their children would only make things worse. In fact, for years the commonly held notion was that children did not notice another person's race unless it was pointed out to them. But recent research indicates that children clearly begin to distinguish skin colors and make judgments based on them even as early as the preschool years. One experiment conducted at the University of Texas by researcher Rebecca Bigler delved into the question of when children begin to notice racial differences. The experiment involved children ages four to five years and was conducted in three preschool classrooms. The children were divided into two groups and randomly given either a blue or red T-shirt. For three weeks, the children wore these T-shirts. The teachers never mentioned the different colors, nor did they ever separate the children based on shirt color. When playing, the students did not self-segregate by shirt color.

PROVIDING THE TOOLS

"The best and only sure way to prevent racism and racial violence is by reaching children and giving them the knowledge and tools they need to understand and respect both difference and inclusion. We would be amazed at the amount of positive change possible in our and their lifetimes."—Yolanda Moses, co-chair of RACE Project and a professor at the University of California Riverside.

Quoted in American Anthropological Association, "Understanding 'Whiteness' and Unlearning Racism," press release, June 18, 2009, www.aaanet.org/issues/press/Understanding-Whiteness-and-Unlearning-Racism.cfm.

Still, when Bigler later asked the children which group was better to belong to, nearly all of them chose their own color. They also said they believed they were smarter than members of the other team. And, while children responded that some of the members of the other team were mean, they said that none of the members of their own team were mean. The children had a clear sense of superiority regarding the other team. "The Reds never showed hatred for Blues," said Bigler. "It was more like, 'Blues are fine, but not as good as us.'"[50] Bigler concluded that children will use readily apparent differences, including skin color, in order to put people into categories and make distinctions between themselves and others.

Even young children notice differences between people and may think their own group is better than those outside of that group.

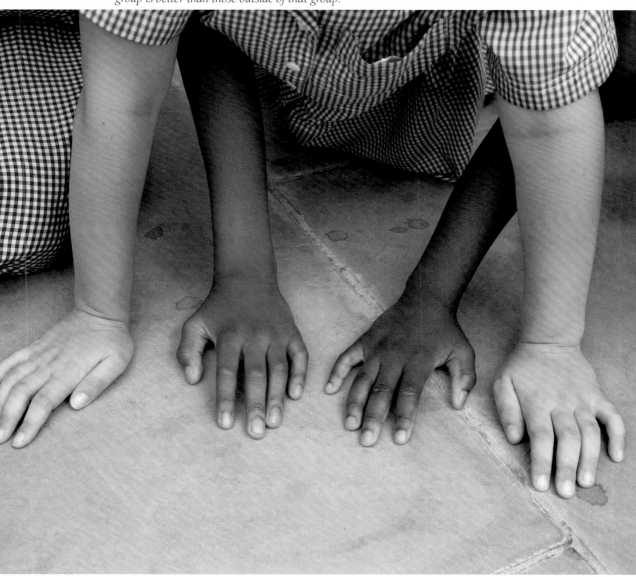

Rodney Southern, a writer and the father of two, agrees that even young children notice race. He says it is important that discussions of race and tolerance "start at a very young age. Kids form ideals very early, and we cannot underestimate the social dangers of waiting."[51]

Racism Free in the Classroom

In addition to parents, teachers are also key figures in shaping a child's attitudes toward others. Just as parents can help prevent racism through discussions of values and tolerance in the home, teachers can also help prevent racism in the classroom. There are many classroom activities in use every day that help raise student awareness of racism. These include more traditional activities, such as reading and responding to poems, short stories, and novels that deal with race and racism around the world. But activities can also include more original learning opportunities, such as writing, acting out skits, or role-playing to allow students to practice responding to racist remarks.

"A COMMUNITY EFFECT"

"Overall, there's not a lot of evidence that, at least in the long term, kids get their prejudice from their parents. I would call it more of a community effect than a parental effect. The community fosters tolerance or prejudice."—Charles Stangor, director of the Laboratory for the Study of Social Stereotyping and Prejudice at the University of Maryland.

Quoted in Sonia Scherr, "It Takes a Village to Raise a Racist," AlterNet, February 9, 2010, www.alternet.org/media/145596/it_takes_a_village_to_raise_a_racist.

One example of ways in which racism is prevented in schools comes from Jefferson Middle School in Eugene, Oregon. In 1986 the school became the nation's first "Racism Free Zone." This means that racism—or any form of discrimination—is not tolerated in the school. In the main hall of the school hangs a plaque with the words "Our school will be free and open to all people without regard to cultural or color differences. No racist remark or harassment will be allowed. Any such actions will result in serious consequences. Our school will be respectful to people of all races and cultures."[52]

In a Racism Free Zone, students and teachers alike receive training in cultural awareness and ways to combat racism. Teachers and other staff attend workshops on racial sensitivity and cross-cultural communication. Students are given an orientation at the beginning of the school year that explains the concept of being racism free. In addition, a number of students are trained as peer mediators and peer counselors and take an active role in peer conflict management. Issues of student diversity are addressed in the classroom through instruction, assessment, and classroom activities and programs. The Racism Free Zone program was so successful at Jefferson that other schools in the nation—as well as banks and even some cities—have adopted it.

Teacher Training

Further efforts to prevent racism in schools include training teachers to recognize incidents of racism and intolerance. Lisa Delpit is an African American educator who has written extensively on the topic of race and culture in the classroom. She explains what is necessary in order for teachers to be effective in preventing bias and racism in schools:

> If we are to successfully educate all of our children, we must work to remove the blinders built of stereotypes, . . . ignorance, social distance, biased research, and racism. We must work to destroy those blinders so that it is possible to really see, to really know the students we must teach. Yes, if we are to be successful at educating diverse children, we must accomplish the Herculean feat of developing this clear-sightedness, for in the words of a wonderful Native Alaskan educator: "In order to teach you, I must know you."[53]

A number of programs exist to raise educators' awareness of issues in diversity and encourage an understanding of a multicultural student body. One such program, developed by the

Primary schools in the United Kingdom asked students to submit pictures for a "say no to racism" campaign. Teachers are trained to be more aware of racism in the classroom and encourage understanding.

Southern Poverty Law Center, is the Teaching Diverse Students Initiative (TDSi). This program aims to help teachers by supplying resources on racial diversity. The primary goal of TDSi is to help improve the quality of teaching for students of color by helping educators improve their skills and understandings in regard to race and ethnicity. Teachers and students alike can visit the TDSi Web site and click through a variety of tools meant to educate and enlighten on the subject of race. One such tool is the Common Beliefs Survey. This survey helps teachers examine thirteen common beliefs that teachers have about meeting the learning needs of their students. Three common beliefs are:

- I don't think of my students in terms of their race or ethnicity; I am color blind when it comes to my teaching.

- The gap in the achievement among students of different races is about poverty, not race.

- Students of different races and ethnicities often have different learning styles, and good teachers will match their instruction to these learning styles.[54]

Teachers can take the survey and then view short videos of respected sociologists and psychologists commenting on the many racial suppositions that people make. One of the experts, Linda Darling-Hammond of Stanford University, is certain that although great progress has been made, much work remains. She rejects the notion that teachers and students can be color-blind. She says, "They will be making assumptions about kids on the basis of race; kids will be making assumptions about teachers. Those are all assumptions that can be tested and debunked and reframed, but you can't get there without understanding that race is part of the context."[55] Furthermore, says Delpit, it is not worthwhile to ignore color. "I would like to suggest," she says, "that if one does not see color, then one does not really see children. Children made 'invisible' in this manner become hard-pressed to see themselves worthy of notice."[56]

Sonia Nieto, a professor at the University of Massachusetts Amherst, uses TDSi and considers it a vital resource for her students and herself. She describes the program as different from a lot of what goes on in teacher education because it asks teachers to really confront their reality and their biases and their misperceptions. And to be brutally honest about what brought them to teaching and about their attitudes about the students who they teach. . . . It's really good because before you can really get to know your students you have to know yourself.[57]

In the Community

Beyond the home and the classroom, racism can also be prevented in the community at large through programs that encourage racial tolerance. People around the world work to improve race relations through discussion groups, community education programs, and other activities. Founded in 1993, Seeds for Peace is an organization that offers programs around the world to help prevent racism by fostering the development of empathy and respect for others. One program is a yearly summer camp in Maine for young people of different races and ethnicities. There, the participants work on a series of team-building activities with the goal of bringing them in close contact with one another so mutual respect and empathy develops.

CREATING TOLERANCE

"Exposure at an early age to a divergence of views plays a crucial part in laying the foundations for tolerance and understanding."—Tony Blair, former prime minister of the United Kingdom.

Quoted in Seeds of Peace, "Testimonials," Seeds of Peace, www.seedsofpeace.org/media/testimonials.

Another organization is the People's Institute for Survival and Beyond. Founded in 1980, the institute trains people to become effective community organizers. More than one hundred thousand people have gone through the institute's Undoing Racism Community Organizing Workshop, where they learn the basic skills necessary to lead anti-racist activities in their own

Campers at Seeds of Peace stand together during a flag-raising ceremony. The program aims to help youth form friendships across national divides.

communities, including effective community organizing, leadership development, coalition building, fundraising, and publicity. Workshops have been conducted in communities in Minnesota, California, New York, Mississippi, and Louisiana.

The People's Institute also conducts a program called Youth Agenda. This program mentors young people in universities and throughout the communities in which the institute is active, helping them learn to recognize and speak out against racism in their own schools and communities.

A number of other nonprofit organizations across the United States and around the world attempt to combat ongoing racism through education. One is A World of Difference Institute, sponsored by the Anti-Defamation League. Founded in Boston, Massachusetts, in 1986, A World of Difference travels the world providing diversity training to businesses as well as schools, universities, and communities. Through individual training programs, videos, discussion groups, and role-playing, A World of Difference Institute helps participants recognize bias, explore diversity, and improve relations between people of different races.

According to one Drexel University student, "each interactive workshop asked students to think critically about their own assumptions [and] . . . they discussed ways that students and faculty could be part of the solution to campus problems."[58]

Making a Difference

Each individual in a community can make a difference in race relations. Carolyn Wagner is one person who has made a difference in a number of ways, starting when she was a child. When Wagner was twelve years old, she witnessed a group of white men—including her father—savagely attack a black man in Booneville, Arkansas. Afterward they tied him to a railroad track. Wagner waited until the men had left, then she quietly drifted to the tracks, pulled out a knife she kept in her boot, and cut the terrified man loose. "That was a turning point," Wagner recalled later. "I felt like I had made a difference when I was able to cut that man free. I realized I can make a choice to

Mother and Son Fight Racism

One day in 1983 in Eugene, Oregon, sixth-grader Zakee Ansari noticed a fellow student drawing a hanging black man next to a burning cross. Zakee watched as the boy gave the drawing to their social studies teacher, who immediately hung it on the wall. Zakee asked the teacher to take the picture down. The teacher agreed, but the same student drew another picture of the same violent image. Again the teacher hung it on the wall. Zakee angrily tore the picture from the wall, ran from the room, and made his way to the principal's office. But the principal refused to do anything.

When Bahati Ansari, Zakee's mother, learned of the episode, she was outraged. But the teacher and principal defended the decision to display the pictures. Ansari eventually convinced the district superintendant to send a letter to all parents and school staff describing and condemning the incident. Ansari went on to develop her own training program called the Racism Free Zone. Two teachers at Jefferson Middle School requested the four-hour training for their classes. The training led to Jefferson Middle becoming the first Racism Free Zone in the nation.

be a passive observer or I can become involved to diminish the harm that they're doing. And that's what I did from that night on, and that's what I'm still doing."[59]

Today Wagner is the cofounder of Families United Against Hate. The nonprofit group counsels people like her whose lives have been affected by traumatic racial violence. By creating a community of survivors, Wagner hopes to provide guidance and forge a greater understanding of racism and the long-term damage it can do.

While community programs such those offered by Families United Against Hate, Seeds of Peace, the People's Institute for Survival and Beyond, and A World of Difference cannot completely end all racism, they can begin an important process. Dialogue between people of different backgrounds and activism can lead to a greater awareness of racism and how to take steps to prevent it in the community.

Prizing Diversity

Another arena in which there have been efforts to prevent racism is the workplace. In 2007 the U.S. Equal Employment Opportunity Commission (EEOC) introduced a nationwide initiative to combat racism. Known as E-RACE, the outreach program helps identify issues that often lead to discrimination and looks at strategies that may work in combating racism in businesses all across the country. Perhaps most importantly, E-RACE tries to bring greater public awareness to the issues of race and color discrimination. By studying race in today's workplace, E-RACE organizers hope to use technology to get a better idea about how prevalent workplace prejudice is and how individual communities might work to eliminate it. According to William Tamayo, a regional attorney for the EEOC in San Francisco, "the E-RACE Initiative urges us to understand and address the multifaceted and complex nature of racism in the 21st century so that discrimination doesn't rob our nation of the contributions that a diverse population can make."[60]

Combating racism often means that a concerted effort must be made to seek diversity when hiring employees. "Most companies have realized that mathematically, they cannot have the best talent available if minorities aren't represented,"[61] says Luke

What Children Notice

Manning Marable is a professor of African American studies at Columbia University in New York who writes extensively on issues of race. Below, he describes how society imposes ideas about race on children and what must be done to change these negative perceptions.

> The racial system in America is something that people, including children, repeatedly and constantly encounter, and frequently find pressing against them. For the most part, whites and blacks still live in essentially parallel racial universes. . . . Our children notice all of this.
>
> Children soon learn that being "different" can be a good or bad thing, depending on how it is classified into the hierarchy that society has established. They compile observations linked with skin color, family background, and language, noticing whether the phenotype or physical appearance of another child is similar to that child's adult guardians or parents. . . . All of these experiences and observations accumulate into categories, which are given validation by parents, teachers, and people in authority.
>
> To change this process of race-making in the minds of young children will require bold, new approaches to early childhood education. We must teach our children that a new world is possible to achieve. Let us imagine that new world through how we teach our children. Let us live that change we want to achieve.

Manning Marable, "How Our Children Learn Racism," American Democracy Project, October 17, 2006, http://ee.iusb.edu/index.php?/adp/blog/how_our_children_learn_racism.

Visconti, chief executive officer of DiversityInc., a diversity management consulting company.

But history professor Jennifer Delton says the quest to hire a diverse workforce can be complex and confusing. Society, she explains, sends us conflicting messages about race and its importance in the workplace and in culture at large. "Diversity experts ask us to hold all of these competing views in our heads at once," she says. "Race matters. Race doesn't matter. It's fluid and

People of all backgrounds live in New York City, generating great diversity and creativity.

invisible, but can also be classified and seen. . . . It is a precarious foundation for fair, effective hiring policies."[62]

Scott E. Page, a professor at the University of Michigan, has spent years researching diversity in the workplace, and he is convinced that an organization's strength lies in its diversity. For Page, productivity, not prejudice, is the focus. "New York City is the perfect example of diversity functioning well," he said in an interview. "It's an exciting place that produces lots of innovation and creativity. It's not a coincidence that New York has so much energy and also so much diversity."[63] Using statistical models, Page has determined that a variety of backgrounds working together often produce a financial boon for a company's bottom line.

"People from different backgrounds have varying ways of looking at problems, what I call 'tools,'" says Page. "The sum of these tools is far more powerful in organizations with diversity than in ones where everyone has gone to the same schools, been trained in the same mold and thinks in almost identical ways."[64]

All of these efforts to prevent racism in the home, in schools, in the workplace, and in the community will determine what racism will look like in the future.

CHAPTER 5

RACISM AND THE FUTURE

Scholars and critics debate the future of racism. Will increased contact between races lead to a greater understanding of one another? Will racism disappear because of better education programs and new, stricter laws against hate crimes and discrimination? Will racism remain a potent force despite all efforts to eradicate it? Even more disturbing is the question of whether gains of the past will be reversed in the future, and whether racism will be joined by a new kind of prejudice toward others.

The Economics of Race

Misunderstandings between people of different races can undermine efforts to deal effectively with racism. In the United States, as in other countries, a failure to understand a person of a different race can often deepen tensions. The recession of 2008 and 2009 highlighted an interesting aspect in the ongoing challenges people of different races have in relating to one another. Politicians and pundits called the recession the worst financial meltdown since the stock market crash of 1929, which led to the Great Depression of the 1930s. Like that earlier crisis, banks stopped lending, people lost their houses, and unemployment spiraled, topping 10 percent. For some people, racial resentment festered as they looked to cast blame not on the poor economic conditions but on people who appeared different.

Yet in the small town of McDonough, located in Henry County, Georgia, the tough times had an unexpected impact on local residents. Instead of deepening the distance between blacks and whites, the economic hardship brought people together. As in so many other parts of the country, people of all

Asian and Hispanic populations in the United States will increase significantly in coming years, creating a more diverse—and perhaps more accepting—population.

colors lost jobs and found themselves standing in unemployment lines and food donation centers together. Black-owned businesses, like A.J.'s Turkey Grill, began attracting white patrons looking for tasty, reasonably priced food. In McDonough whites and blacks began to interact more, to talk to one another, and to help each other get through the hard times. *New York Times* reporter Shaila Dewan observed, "The idea that the recession is an equalizer has become accepted in Henry County."[65]

The all-white Henry County government had tried in the past to bring diversity to its ranks, but until the crisis nothing worked. "There used to be a lot of racial tension here," says Eugene Edwards, president of the local National Association for the Advancement of Colored People (NAACP), "but everybody knows that we need each other to survive this recession."[66] What remains unclear is how the community will respond once the downturn lifts. The shared hardship may be a bridge to greater racial harmony in the future, or old habits and divisions may return once the economy stabilizes, or rebounds.

Places like McDonough, Georgia, may provide a glimpse of what society could be like in the future. According to the U.S. Census Bureau, white people will cease being the majority race in 2050. The projection, adjusted after the worldwide recession of 2008 and 2009, is based on birth and death rates, as well as a slower pace of immigration into the country. By 2050 whites will account for 49 percent of the population; blacks will make up 12.2 percent—little changed from 2009 figures. The Asian population will increase from 4.4 percent to 6 percent. Most dramatically, the Hispanic population will rise from 15 percent to 28 percent of the U.S. population. Inevitably, racial and ethnic tolerance and acceptance will be tested across the nation, both in small towns and in larger cities.

The Obama Factor

President Barack Obama, as the first black president in U.S. history, may have an impact on the future of race relations in the United States. Melissa Harris-Lacewell, an associate professor of politics and African American studies at Princeton University in New Jersey, believes that change has already occurred. She writes,

> As citizens in a democracy, we can choose the future of our racial politics. Not all at once and not without struggle, but we can make new choices. And this time, African-Americans participate in the process of remaking America's racial story from a very different position than we have occupied in the past. Rather than being solely on the margins of national power, black Americans, through the person of Obama, have achieved a new kind of citizenship more empowered to recreate American race.[67]

Despite Harris-Lacewell's optimism, some of Obama's supporters voice frustration with the president. His policies, they claim, differ little from his predecessors. "There was an expectation," writes columnist Charles M. Blow, "particularly among African Americans, that the first African American president would at least be vocal about feeling their pain. I think that has not been the case. . . . He said he's not going to focus separately on African American issues at all. That let a lot of people down."[68]

President Barack Obama makes a speech as Vice President Joe Biden listens in the background. Many people are optimistic that Obama will do much to improve race relations in the United States, while others look for signs of favoritism.

Other Americans bristle at the very idea of any president playing favorites on the subjects of race and ethnicity. The notion itself, they suggest, is racist; Obama is the president of all Americans. But in the short term, as Harris-Lacewell points out, "the election of a black president has not changed the material realities of racial inequality. African-Americans are significantly more distressed than their white counterparts on every meaningful economic indicator: income, unemployment, wealth, education, home ownership and home foreclosures."[69] Asking one man to fix all of that may be asking too much.

Race Plays No Role

For many Americans today, race plays no role in their opinions or decisions about other people. Just ask Setti Warren. In November 2009 Warren was elected the first African American mayor of Newton, Massachusetts. The town's population is eighty-three thousand, and only 3 percent are African Americans. To get elected, Warren had to win the white vote in large numbers, and he did just that, in part by knocking on eleven thousand doors and introducing himself. He believes that race played no role in his victory. "I'm actually really proud of that," says Warren. "People were willing to look beyond race in making their decision, and that's a tribute to Newton and its progressive nature."[70]

Warren's impressive background is itself progressive and service oriented. His father is a university administrator in Chicago, Illinois, who worked in presidential politics in the 1980s; his mother is a retired social worker. Warren once headed the New England branch of the Federal Emergency Management Agency (FEMA) and worked for both President Bill Clinton and Senator John Kerry. He spent a year in Iraq as a navy intelligence officer.

As mayor, Warren faces a small mountain of problems, including a budget crisis and the possibility of raising taxes to pay for a new, state-of-the-art high school. His success or failure at solving these problems will have nothing to do with the color of his skin.

Civil rights leader Andrew Young discusses his experience taking a DNA-based genealogy test. These tests can reveal a person's exact racial makeup and may reveal that racial lines are more blurred than they appear.

Changing Perceptions of Race

Anthropologist Nina Jablonski envisions a future in which color remains a fact of life, but fewer distinctions based on color exist. One thousand years from now, she says, people "will still come in lots of colors, but in big cities, where many people from different places live and mix, there will be even more who have 'in-between' skin colors and fewer people with strikingly dark or light complexions."[71]

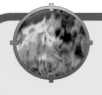

Changing Its 'Toon: Disney's First Black Heroine

Ever since Snow White first fell in love with Prince Charming in 1937, the faces of Disney heroines have been almost uniformly white. Then in 1995, the film studio released *Pocahontas*, based on the real Pocahontas, a Native American who made friends with British explorers. In 1998 came *Mulan*, the story of Mulan, a young Chinese maiden, and in 2002 the studio released *Lilo & Stitch*, a movie about a precocious Hawaiian girl (Lilo) and her pet (Stitch). Then Disney animators created a story set in New Orleans, Louisiana, and felt it only natural that the main character be African American. Released in 2009, *The Princess and the Frog* features Tiana, a young black girl who dreams of owning a jazz club. "It is a universal story," codirector John Musker says. "It is a story of trying to follow your dreams and overcoming obstacles. And I don't think that necessarily knows a certain color." The racial breakthrough has had different effects on different generations. One *Chicago Tribune* columnist commented that middle-aged black women saw the film as an important turning point in racial progress. But black parents, she said, noticed that the significance of Tiana's race is lost on many young children.

Quoted in Mike Cidoni, "New 'Toon Continues Disney Trend Toward Diversity," ABC News, December 2, 2009, http://abcnews.go.com/Entertainment/wireStory?id=9231867.

Anika Noni Rose, star of Disney's The Princess and the Frog, *attends the movie's premiere. This is the first Disney movie to put a black character in the lead.*

Complexion, or skin tone, is already a complicated phenomenon. People who identify themselves as white may have genetically darker skin than many whites, whereas self-identifying blacks may appear lighter than many whites. Scholar Henry Louis Gates Jr. is convinced that *race* is a relative term. All people, he suggests, are of mixed race, products of a complicated history. DNA tests that can determine the exact percentage of a person's racial makeup, he says, will prove this fact in the years to come. "The more we use DNA tests to trace our family trees, the more we're going to discover just how tangled our roots really are," says Gates. "We are all mulattoes [biracial people] of one kind or another. In the end, what actually makes us black or white? Or have those terms become outdated?"[72]

The answer to Gates's question may lie within the recent work of geneticists. Scientists have mapped the human genome, the complex code of human life, and determined that all human beings are genetically the same. Race, therefore, is simply a social construction with no basis in science. Any differences between races are likely a result of historical developments, such as wars, slavery, migration patterns, and agriculture. In tracing human history to its very roots, scientists have also concluded that all human beings originated on the African continent some two hundred thousand years ago. Thus, a common ancestor connects all of humanity. How then did the various skin colors evolve? According to biological anthropologist Alan Goodman, "all skin colors, whether light or dark, are not due to race but to adaptation for life under the sun."[73]

Despite the scientific proof that racial differences are genetically meaningless, some people will remain convinced that "black" and "white" are categories that can be used to understand human behavior, morality, or intelligence. In the United States and other countries around the world, defining people by the color of their skin is a kind of shorthand by which people are viewed and often judged, for better and for worse. "You are what you have to defend," says actor Don Cheadle. "Cause it doesn't matter that I'm 19% European and 81% African. In America, I have to deal with the problems that black people in America have."[74]

School Desegregation

Some people worry that racism may increase in the future if schools do not remain racially integrated. American schools legally separated blacks from whites until the 1954 *Brown v. Board of Education* Supreme Court decision made the practice illegal. But since 1991 more than one hundred school districts have fought and won the right to have their desegregation orders overturned in the courts on the grounds that such a requirement puts undue financial burdens on them. They argue that forced integration has already had the desired positive effect and is no longer necessary or reasonable. Some critics, though, fear that if white and black students are no longer forced to interact, racism may grow.

Race and Genetic Tests

For many people the future of race and racism may begin with a simple blood test. DNA Tribes and Ethnoancestry are two of the companies that sell over-the-counter products that help a person discover his or her racial and ethnic heritage. Costing between $99 and $250, these tests may do more than simply satisfy a curiosity. Verifying a student's race may make him or her eligible for race-based college admission. Alan Moldawer's two adopted sons, Matt and Andrew, took the test and discovered that they were 11 percent northern African. Their father says he will not hesitate to use the DNA information to apply for financial aid.

For Pearl Duncan, the genetic test forced her to reevaluate herself and her background. While most Westerners would identify her as a black woman, Duncan found out that she is 10 percent Scottish on her mother's side. Contacting her Scottish relatives was about making peace with the past before moving on with her life. "By acknowledging me," she says, "the Scots are beginning to acknowledge that these guys were slaveholders." Duncan knows that while racial differences may be only skin deep, they still matter in a world that still sees and judges based on race.

Quoted in Amy Harmon, "Seeking Ancestry in DNA Ties Uncovered by Tests," *New York Times,* April 12, 2006, www.nytimes.com/2006/04/12/us/12genes.html?pagewanted=1&_r=1.

School desegregation came to a head in 2007 when the Supreme Court addressed the issue. In a 5–4 decision, the Court ruled to stop race-based assignments of children to public schools. The ruling sent shock waves across the nation, angering those who believe that forced desegregation remained necessary. According to legal analyst Jeffrey Toobin, "what this court said was even though only a few slots were determined by race, that's too many. You just simply can't consider race in deciding which school kids go to."[75]

"CLOSING THE RACIAL GAP"

"At some point, this has to move beyond a 'do the right thing white people' discussion and become a 'this is for the good of America' discussion. We have to start convincing people that closing the racial gap helps everyone."—Ta-Nehisi Coates, newspaper columnist.

Ta-Nehisi Coates, "The Issue Is Black and White," TPMCAFÉ, March 31, 2008, http://tpm cafe.talkingpointsmemo.com/2008/03/31/the_issue_is_black_and_white.

Crystal Meredith welcomed the high court's decision. She had sued her son's public school district, which had denied the boy's attendance at a school close to their home and forced him to take a three-hour bus ride to attend a school farther away. Meredith, a white woman, along with a group of black parents, complained that this kind of forced integration was no longer necessary. "We are here not because we didn't get our first choice, but because we got no choice," says Meredith. "I was told by the school board that my son's education was not as important as their plan. I was told I should sacrifice his learning in order to maintain the status quo."[76]

Rita Jones Turner does not agree that forced integration is no longer necessary. In 1970 she became one of the first black students at Vestavia Hills High School in Birmingham, Alabama, after forced desegregation. She remembers that often the school bus would not stop on her street; when it did and she arrived at school, she was placed into remedial classes, while at lunchtime white students harassed her by tearing barrettes from her hair.

Thirty-six years later Jones Turner received a note from her old school informing her of its attempt to change the policy of desegregation and force her ninth-grade son to enroll elsewhere. Specifically, the school district filed a court motion to stop forced integration. Jones Turner's own experience at Vestavia remains a painful memory, but she resents any attempts at turning back the clock on progress. "We were used, mistreated, downtrodden, and discriminated against," says Jones Turner. "I have no problem with being a sacrificial lamb for the good of the community, but to have the system back out now is not fair. They made a commitment to educate black children."[77]

THE FUTURE OF RACISM

"The [task] . . . is to make white culture—the dominant cultural form on the planet today—the problem, the enemy, not only of folks of color, but of whites too. It is to demonstrate that white supremacy is not only homicidal to the black and brown but suicidal to those of us who are members of the club that created it."— Tim Wise, antiracism activist.

Tim Wise, "Paleness as Pathology: The Future of Racism and Anti-Racism in America," *LIP Magazine*, May 2006, www.lipmagazine.org/~timwise/palepathology.html.

The Vestavia school board denies any racial motivation in wanting to halt integration; instead, the board claims that economics forced their decision. The school's budget can no longer bear the strain of busing black students from all the way across town.

The possibility that integration in schools will no longer be enforced has many people worried that there will be a resurgence of racists and racism. These are both factors that must be addressed if schools—and societies at large—are ever to get beyond race. Gilberto Sabá, Brazil's secretary of state for human rights from 2000 to 2001, believes that the international community

The plaintiffs in the Brown v. Board of Education *case. The case banned segregation in schools.*

must first address racism of the past before moving forward. "Slavery has been a tragedy for millions of people for centuries and continues to have consequences," said Sabá. "It doesn't mean we have to remain locked in the past, but we need to understand that past to address the present and to address the future."[78]

More than half a century after *Brown v. Board of Education* desegregated American schools, many are wondering whether the ruling will still play a role in the future or if it is simply a relic of a time when racism was far more prevalent than it is today.

Replacing Racism

Is racism disappearing? That is a question many people are asking. Some people, including Jablonski, predict that in the future, with the increasing numbers of interracial couples and biracial children, the two races may well gradually blend into one. Whether or not everyone will eventually belong to a single race is debatable, but the fact remains that as people of different races continue to interact with each other, old racist ideas and attitudes will give way to a greater understanding of one another. And that could signal the demise of racism.

CHANGING THE ENVIRONMENT

"I don't think what's in people's heads is going to change until the environment that places these things in their head has changed."—Anthony Greenwald, professor of psychology at the University of Washington.

Quoted in Elizabeth Landau, "You May Be More Racist than You Think, Study Says," CNN.com, April 2, 2009, http://edition.cnn.com/2009/HEALTH/01/07/racism.study /index.html.

Already an increasing awareness of the effects of racial prejudice and discrimination has led to a lessening of the powerful racism of the past. And some people believe that as the issue of bias against others based on race continues to fade, the next wave of global prejudice may be aimed at those professing particular beliefs. Rather than racial divisions, the future may be one in which the importance of skin color recedes while religious differences take prominence. Race expert George M. Fredrickson says, "Race offers less of a haven to the alienated and disenchanted than it once did, because of the worldwide campaign against it that was one of the great achievements of the twentieth century. But absolutist religion retains its appeal, and . . . has the potential to become the twenty-first century's principal source of intergroup conflict and aggression."[79]

Fredrickson's words are echoed in the global fight against religious extremism. They are also seen in the waves of violence aimed at people of varying religious beliefs. An incident in Dresden, Germany, provides a glimpse into one possible future. With a massive influx of immigrants, racially motivated crimes in that city rose 6.3 percent between 2007 and 2009. One of the most vicious crimes was the July 2009 murder of Egyptian pharmacist Marwa al-Sherbini. She was stabbed to death in a courtroom by Russian-born German Alex Wiens. Al-Sherbini had testified that Wiens called her a terrorist at a local park. Al-Sherbini's head scarf apparently compelled Wiens to insult her for being Muslim. Wiens attacked al-Sherbini during the court proceedings, stabbing her eighteen times in front of her three-year-old son, her husband, and everyone in the courtroom before being subdued.

Egyptian pharmacist Marwa al-Sherbini was stabbed to death by a man who called her a terrorist because she wore a head scarf.

Whether religious prejudice will replace racial prejudice remains unclear. Yet for victims of racial or religious prejudice alike, justice may never be entirely possible without a commitment to creating laws that protect people from discrimination. And while no law can legislate attitudes and fears, there is hope that the struggle for racial progress will continue well into the twenty-first century and beyond. Civil rights leader Martin Luther King Jr. spoke of patience and persistence in such a fight when he said, "The arc of history is long, but it bends toward justice."[80]

Introduction: "All Things Are Possible"

1. Quoted in CNNPolitics.com, "Transcript: 'This Is Your Victory,' Says Obama," CNNPolitics.com, November 4, 2008, http://edition.cnn.com/2008/POLITICS/11/04/obama.transcript.
2. Quoted in Asian News International, "Obama's Victory Marks End of Racism: S. African Nobel Laureate," Thaindian News, November 11, 2008, www.thaindian.com/news portal/india-news/obamas-victory-marks-end-of-racism-safrican-nobel-laureate _100117532.html.
3. Quoted in CNN.com, "Obama: Nobel Peace Prize in 'Call to Action,'" CNN.com, October 9, 2009, www.cnn.com/2009/WORLD/europe/10/09/nobel.peace.prize.
4. Molefi Kete Asante, *Erasing Racism: The Survival of the African Nation*. Amherst: New York: Prometheus, 2003, p. 194.
5. Asante, *Erasing Racism*, p. 8.
6. Robert Chrisman and Ernest Allen Jr., "Ten Reasons: A Response to David Horowitz," University of Massachusetts Amherst, www.umass.edu/afroam/hor.html.

Chapter 1: Racism Today

7. Quoted in Beverly Daniel Tatum, *"Why Are All the Black Kids Sitting Together in the Cafeteria?" And Other Conversations About Race*. New York: Basic Books, 1999, p. 7.
8. Quoted in James Verini, "Stopping the Next McVeigh," Daily Beast, November 7, 2009, www.thedailybeast.com/blogs-and-stories/2009-11-07/stopping-the-next-mcveigh.
9. Quoted in Katya Adler, "Spain Reflects on Football Racism Row," BBC News, November 18, 2004, http://news.bbc.co.uk/2/hi/europe/4024167.stm.
10. Quoted in Adler, "Spain Reflects on Football Racism Row."

11. Quoted in Adler, "Spain Reflects on Football Racism Row."
12. Quoted in Rachel Donadio, "Race Riots Grip Italian Town, and Mafia Is Suspected," *New York Times*, January 10, 2010, www.nytimes.com/2010/01/11/world/europe/11italy.html?e mc=eta1.
13. Quoted in Dan Gilgoff, "Investing in Diversity," *U.S. News & World Report*, November 1, 2009, p. 72.
14. Clarence Otis Jr., interview by Ed Gordon, *News and Notes*, National Public Radio, April 11, 2006, www.npr.org/tem plates/story/story.php?storyId=5336052.
15. Quoted in Annette Walker, "Black and Latino Workers Win $21 Million Discrimination Lawsuit Against Parks Dept.," *New Amsterdam News*, April 17–23, 2008.
16. Quoted in Ronnie Polaneczky, "A Splash of Cold Water," Philly.com, July 9, 2009.
17. Quoted in Zoe Tillman and Max Stendahl, "Montco Swim Club Accused of Racial Discrimination," Philly.com, July 9, 2009, www.philly.com/philly/news/year-in-review/50341 552.html?userLogout=y.
18. Quoted in Elizabeth Landau, "You May Be More Racist than You Think, Study Says," CNN.com, April 2, 2009, http:// edition.cnn.com/2009/HEALTH/01/07/racism.study.
19. Asante, *Erasing Racism*, p. 254.
20. William Julius Wilson, *More than Just Race: Being Black and Poor in the Inner City*. New York: Norton, 2009, p. 1.

Chapter 2: What Motivates Racism?

21. Tatum, *"Why Are All the Black Kids Sitting Together in the Cafeteria?"*, pp. 3–4.
22. American Psychological Association, "Racism and Psychology," American Psychological Association, www.apa.org/pi /oema/resources/brochures/racism.aspx.
23. American Psychological Association, "Racism and Psychology."
24. Quoted in David A. Harris, "The Stories, the Statistics, and the Law: Why 'Driving While Black' Matters," University of Dayton School of Law, 1999, http://academic.udayton.edu /race/03justice/dwb01.htm.

25. Quoted in Dayo Olopede, "Skip Gates Speaks," The Root, July 21, 2009, www.theroot.com/views/skip-gates-speaks? page=0,1.

26. Quoted in Cambridge Police Department Incident Report #9005127, July 16, 2009, www.thebostonchannel.com/down load/2009/0720/20120754.pdf.

27. Quoted in Helene Cooper and Abby Goodnough, "Over Beers, No Apologies, but Plans to Have Lunch," *New York Times*, July 30, 2009, www.nytimes.com/2009/07/31/us /politics31obama.html.

28. Quoted in Cooper and Goodnough, "Over Beers, No Apologies, but Plans to Have Lunch."

29. Malcolm Gladwell, *Blink*. New York: Little, Brown, 2005, p. 143.

Chapter 3: Fighting Racism

30. Lyndon B. Johnson, "To Fulfill These Rights," commencement address, Howard University, Washington, DC, June 4, 1965, www.lbjlib.utexas.edu/johnson/archives.hom/speeches .hom/650604.asp.

31. Quoted in Linda Greenhouse, *Becoming Justice Blackmun: Harry Blackmun's Supreme Court Journey*. New York: Times Books, 2005, p. 133.

32. Ross Douthat, "Race in 2028," *New York Times*, July 19, 2009, www.nytimes.com/2009/07/20/opinion/20douthat.html.

33. Quoted in Joseph Williams and Matt Negrin, "Affirmative Action Foes Point to Obama," *Boston Globe*, March 18, 2008, www.boston.com/news/nation/articles/2008/03/18/affirmative _action_foes_point_to_obama.

34. Quoted in Williams and Negrin, "Affirmative Action Foes Point to Obama."

35. Glenn C. Loury, interview by Bill Moyers, *Bill Moyers Journal*, PBS, June 20, 2008, www.pbs.org/moyers/journal/0620 2008/transcript3.html.

36. Quoted in Lisa Delpit, *Other People's Children: Cultural Conflict in the Classroom*. New York: New Press, 2006, p. 116.

37. S. Mary Wills, "Workplace Racism Isn't a Stand Alone Issue," The Black Factor, January 3, 2008, http://theblackfactor

.blogspot.com/2008/01/workplace-racism-isnt-stand-alone-issue.html.

38. Quoted in Charlie Savage, "Report Examines Civil Rights During Bush Years," *New York Times*, December 3, 2009, www.nytimes.com/2009/12/03/us/politics/03rights.html.

39. Quoted in Ellis Cose, "The GOP's Civil-Rights Problem," *Newsweek*, December 10, 2009, www.newsweek.com/id/226382.

40. Quoted in U.S. Equal Employment Opportunity Commission, "EEOC Sues Spartan Plumbing for Race Harassment," press release, October 1, 2009, www.eeoc.gov/eeoc/newsroom/release/10-1-09l.cfm.

41. Quoted in U.S. Equal Employment Opportunity Commission, "EEOC Sues Spartan Plumbing for Race Harassment."

42. Shankar Vedantam, "Shades of Prejudice," *New York Times*, January 18, 2010, www.nytimes.com/2010/01/19/opinion/19vedantam.html.

43. Edward Telles, "Racial Discrimination and Miscegenation: The Experience in Brazil," *UN Chronicle*, November 3, 2007.

44. Muna Al-Fuzai, "Don't Be Ashamed of Your Dark Skin," *Kuwait Times*, June 11, 2008, www.kuwaittimes.net/read_news.php?newsid=Mjk2OTczODUy.

45. Quoted in Huffington Post, "Robert Mugabe: White Farmers Must Vacate Their Land," Huffington Post, February 28, 2009, www.huffingtonpost.com/2009/02/28/robert-mugabe-white-farme_n_170752.html.

46. Quoted in Nkepile Mabuse, "Desperation Stalks Zimbabwe's White Farmers," CNN.com, September 23, 2009, http://edition.cnn.com/2009/WORLD/africa/09/22/zimbabwe.farmers.

Chapter 4: Preventing Racism

47. Quoted in American Anthropological Association, "Lived Experience," RACE Project, www.understandingrace.com/lived.

48. Anti-Racist Alliance Trust, "Our Children and Anti-Racism," www.antiracistalliance.org.uk/?page_id=19.

49. Quoted in Po Bronson and Ashley Merryman, "See Baby

Discriminate," *Newsweek*, September 14, 2009, www
.newsweek.com/id/214989/page/1.

50. Quoted in Bronson and Merryman, "See Baby Discriminate."

51. Rodney Southern, "How to Prevent Racism in Your Child,"
Associated Content, October 17, 2007, www.associatedcon
tent.com/article/407029/how_to_prevent_racism_in_your_
child.html?cat=25.

52. Quoted in Ed Kent, "Jefferson Middle School: A Racism Free
Zone in Eugene, OR," May 17, 2007, Blogger News Net-
work, www.bloggernews.net/16845.

53. Delpit, *Other People's Children*, pp. 182–83.

54. Teaching Tolerance, "Commonly Held Beliefs That Influence Teachers' Work with Diverse Students," Teaching Tolerance, www.tolerance.org/tdsi/cb_intro.

55. Quoted in Teaching Tolerance, "The Teaching Diverse Students Initiative," 2009, www.tolerance.org/tdsi/.

56. Delpit, *Other People's Children*, p. 177.

57. Quoted in Teaching Tolerance, "The Teaching Diverse Students Initiative."

58. Quoted in Anti-Defamation League, "A World of Difference
Institute: A Campus of Difference," www.adl.org/educa
tion/edu_awod/awod_campus.asp.

59. Quoted in Sonia Scherr, "It Takes a Village to Raise a Racist,"
AlterNet, February 9, 2010.

60. Quoted in U.S. Equal Employment Opportunity Commission, "EEOC Takes a New Approach to Fighting Racism and
Colorism in the 21st Century Workplace," press release,
February 28, 2007, www.eeoc.gov/eeoc/newsroom/re
lease/2-28-07.cfm.

61. Quoted in Gilgoff, "Investing in Diversity," p. 73.

62. Jennifer Delton, "Why Diversity for Diversity's Sake Won't
Work," *Chronicle of Higher Education*, September 28, 2007,
pp. B32–B33.

63. Quoted in Claudia Dreifus, "In Professor's Model, Diversity
= Productivity," *New York Times*, January 8, 2008, www.ny
times.com/2008/01/08/science/08conv.html.

64. Quoted in Dreifus, "In Professor's Model, Diversity = Productivity."

Chapter 5: Racism and the Future

65. Shaila Dewan, "A Racial Divide Is Bridged by Recession, *New York Times*, November 16, 2009, www.nytimes.com /2009/11/17/us/17county.html?_r=1.

66. Quoted in Dewan, "A Racial Divide Is Bridged by Recession."

67. Melissa Harris-Lacewell, "Commentary: Racial Progress Is Far from Finished," CNN.com, June 5, 2009, http://edi tion.cnn.com/2009/LIVING/07/07/lacewell.post.racial/index .html.

68. Quoted in Lloyd Grove, "Are Blacks Abandoning Obama?" Daily Beast, December 15, 2009, www.thedailybeast.com /blogs-and-stories/2009-12-15/has-obama-abandoned-blacks.

69. Harris-Lacewell, "Commentary."

70. Quoted in Abby Goodnough, "History Made, Mayor-Elect Focuses on Local Issues," *New York Times*, December 22, 2009, www.nytimes.com/2009/12/23/us/politics/23warren .html?emc=eta1.

71. Quoted in American Anthropological Association, "Only Skin Deep," RACE Project, www.understandingrace.com /humvar/skin_03.html.

72. Quoted in Ashlinn Quinn, "Rationalizing Race in U.S. History," *African American Lives 2*, PBS, www.pbs.org/wnet /aalives/teachers/rationalizing_race.html.

73. Quoted in American Anthropological Association, "Only Skin Deep."

74. Quoted in Quinn, "Rationalizing Race in U.S. History."

75. Quoted in Bill Mears, "Divided Court Rejects School Diversity Plans," CNN.com, June 28, 2007, http://edition .cnn.com/2007/LAW/06/28/scotus.race.

76. Quoted in Mears, "Divided Court Rejects School Diversity Plans."

77. Quoted in Jenny Jarvie, "School Seeks to End Racial Integration," *Boston Globe*, October 29, 2006, www.boston .com/news/education/k_12/articles/2006/10/29/school_seeks _to_end_racial_integration.

78. Quoted in OnlineNewsHour Extra, "Stopping Racism," On-

lineNewsHour Extra, www.pbs.org/newshour/extra/features /unracism/topstory.html.

79. George M. Fredrickson, *Racism: A Short History*. Princeton, NJ: Princeton University Press, 2003, p. 150.
80. Quoted in William L. Taylor, *The Passion of My Times: An Advocate's Fifty-Year Journey in the Civil Rights Movement*. New York: Da Capo, 2004, p. 219.

Chapter 1: Racism Today

1. According to the author, what is "racism?"
2. How many cases of racial discrimination were filed with the U.S. Equal Employment Opportunity Commission in 2007?
3. Explain the findings of Marianne Bertrand and Dean Karlan in their study on racial discrimination in hiring practices.
4. Describe some of the everyday prejudice experienced by many African Americans as reported by Molefi Kete Asante.

Chapter 2: What Motivates Racism?

1. According to the author, what are some of the ways in which stereotypes can be harmful to people?
2. Explain what Stephen Jay Gould and other scientists mean when they argue that race is genetically meaningless.
3. According to the author, how does racial profiling contribute to racism?
4. Explain what the Implicit Association Test has discovered about bias in blacks and whites.

Chapter 3: Fighting Racism

1. Why do critics of affirmative action sometimes refer to it as reverse discrimination?
2. Explain why Thomas Pettigrew and Joanne Martin believe that "the modern forms of prejudice frequently remain invisible even to its perpetrators."
3. Explain what Harvard scholar and journalist Shankar Vedantam means by "colorism."
4. Explain why the government of Zimbabwe is seizing land from white farmers and redistributing it to blacks.

Chapter 4: Preventing Racism

1. What did a 2007 study published in the *Journal of Marriage and Family* discover about the percentage of parents who discuss race with their children?
2. Explain the Racism Free Zone that began at Jefferson Middle School.
3. Why does Lisa Delpit say it is not worthwhile to ignore color?
4. How does Scott E. Page believe diversity benefits companies?

Chapter 5: Racism and the Future

1. How did the recent global recession affect the interactions between people of different races in McDonough, Georgia?
2. According to Charles M. Blow, why are some African Americans disappointed in President Obama?
3. Explain anthropologist Nina Jablonski's vision of the future.
4. According to the author, why are many American school districts attempting to reverse desegregation laws?

ORGANIZATIONS TO CONTACT

Amnesty International
Easton St.
London, WC1X 0DW, UK
Phone: 44-20-74135500
Web site: www.amnesty.org

Amnesty International is a worldwide organization that campaigns for internationally recognized human rights for all. The organization's 2.2 million supporters work to end injustice and to improve human rights through campaigning and international solidarity.

Human Rights Watch
350 Fifth Ave., 34th Floor
New York, NY 10118
Phone: (212) 290-4700
Web site: www.hrw.org

As one of the world's leading independent defenders and protectors of human rights, Human Rights Watch works to focus international attention where human rights are being violated.

National Association for the Advancement of Colored People (NAACP)
4805 Mt. Hope Dr.
Baltimore, MD 21215
Phone: (877) NAACP-98
Web site: www.naacp.org

Founded in 1909, the NAACP has championed social justice and fought for the civil rights of African Americans for more than a century. It is the oldest, largest, and most widely recognized civil rights organization in the United States.

The People's Institute for Survival and Beyond
601 N. Carrollton
New Orleans, LA 70119
Phone: (504) 301-9292
Web site: www.pisab.org
This national and international collective of antiracist, multicultural community organizers and educators is dedicated to building an effective movement for social transformation through its Undoing Racism and Community Organizing workshops. The institute helps individuals, communities, organizations, and institutions address the causes of racism in order to create a more just and equitable society.

Southern Poverty Law Center (SPLC)
400 Washington Ave.
Montgomery, AL 36104
Phone: (334) 956-8200
Web site: www.splcenter.org
Founded in 1971, the SPLC is internationally known for its tolerance education programs, its legal victories against white supremacists, and its tracking of hate groups. The SPLC fights all forms of discrimination and works to protect society's most vulnerable members. It has achieved significant legal victories, including landmark Supreme Court decisions, against hate groups.

Books

Tonya Bolden, *Tell All the Children Our Story: Memories and Mementos of Being Young and Black in America*. New York: Abrams, 2001. This beautiful book is full of vintage photos and illustrations depicting life for African Americans from the time of slavery to the early twenty-first century. The text draws on the recollections of those who experienced the highs and lows of being black in America.

W.E.B. Du Bois, *The Souls of Black Folk*. New York: Simon & Schuster, 2005. Originally published in 1903, this classic collection of essays by American educator and writer W.E.B. Du Bois looks closely at the interactions and relationships between blacks and whites and offers a solution to the problem of inequality. Du Bois's ideas became the foundation of the modern civil rights movement.

James W. Loewen, *Sundown Towns: A Hidden Dimension of American Racism*. New York: Touchstone, 2006. Between 1890 and 1968 the term "sundown town" became a notorious part of the American experience, especially in the North. They were hamlets, large and small, in which people of color were unwelcome after dark. Author James Loewen collects stories of these racist places and wonders whether any remain in existence today.

Tim Wise, *Between Barack and a Hard Place: Racism and White Denial in the Age of Obama*. San Francisco: City Lights, 2009. In this book author Tim Wise takes a look at the United States in the wake of Barack Obama's election to the presidency. He is quick to dismiss the idea of a post-racial world; instead, he reminds readers of the entrenched racism that remains and the challenges that must be faced to overcome it.

Web Sites

RACE: Are We So Different? (www.understandingrace.com). Developed by the American Anthropological Association, this is the Web site of the RACE Project, which explains the differences among people and reveals the reality and unreality of race. The interactive site includes a brief film on the evolution of race in America, an interactive time line, and articles on the science of race.

RACE: The Power of an Illusion (www.pbs.org/race/000_General /000_00-Home.htm). This well-organized companion site to the documentary film *RACE: The Power of an Illusion* contains online activities and interviews with scholars.

Racism Review (www.racismreview.com). This Web site posts articles, reviews, and commentary about race and race relations in the United States. It also offers an extensive list of race-themed documentaries, a collection of college course syllabi on the subject, and the latest polls and surveys gauging Americans' views on race and racism.

Teaching Tolerance (www.tolerance.org). This Web site is a project of the Southern Poverty Law Center, a civil rights organization. It features a wide range of resources that encourage understanding and acceptance between races.

INDEX

PICTURE CREDITS

Cover, © Jim West/Alamy
AP Images, 16, 18, 33, 35, 52, 71, 75, 83
Andrew Milligan/PA Wire/AP Images, 68
Gale, Cengage Learning, 19, 53
© Bettmann/Corbis, 44
© Françoise Demulder/Corbis, 62
© Will & Deni McIntyre/Corbis, 78–79
© Gideon Mendel/Corbis, 60, 65
© Tim Pannell/Corbis, 26
© Shawn Thew/epa/Corbis, 9
© Stefan Zaklin/epa/Corbis, 50
© Jamil Bittar/Reuters/Corbis, 55
© Brooks Kraft/Sygma/Corbis, 57
Hulton Archive/Getty Images, 13
Mario Tama/Getty Images, 21
Alex Wong/Getty Images, 47
Nicholas Kamm/AFP/Getty Images, 23
Saul Loeb/AFP/Getty Images, 39
Mike Theiler-Pool/Getty Images, 81
Norbert Millauer/AFP/Getty Images, 91
© Benkey JpegFoto/Picture Group via Getty Images, 84
Carl Iwasaki/Time Life Pictures/Getty Images, 89
ullstein bild/The Granger Collection, New York, 29
Epic/The Kobal Collection/The Picture Desk, Inc., 40

ABOUT THE AUTHOR

David Robson's books for young people include *The Murder of Emmett Till*, *The Israeli-Palestinian Conflict*, *Auschwitz*, and *The Black Arts Movement*. He is also a playwright, whose work for the stage has been performed across the United States and abroad. Robson holds a master of fine arts degree from Goddard College, a master of science degree from Saint Joseph's University, and a bachelor of arts degree from Temple University. He lives with his family in Wilmington, Delaware.